Villages of Glasgow
Volume 2

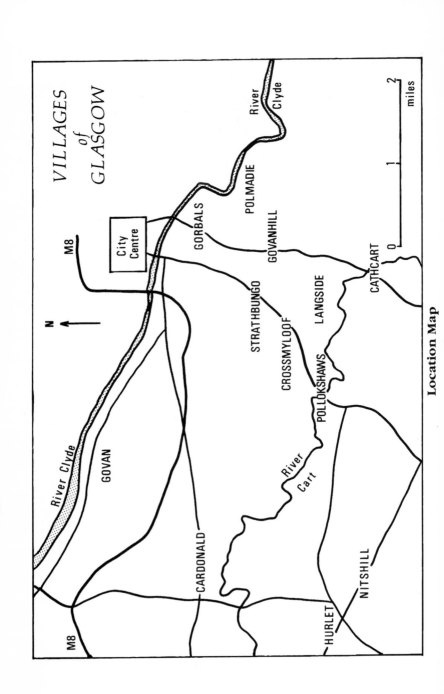

VILLAGES of GLASGOW

Location Map

Villages of Glasgow
Volume 2

AILEEN SMART

JOHN DONALD PUBLISHERS LTD
EDINBURGH

ISBN 0 85976 391 9

British Library Cataloguing in Publication Data.
A catalogue record for this book is available from the British Library.

The publisher acknowledges subsidy from the Scottish Arts Council
towards the publication of this volume.

For Katherine

PostScript Typesetting & Origination by Brinnoven, Livingston.
Printed & bound in Great Britain by Bell & Bain Ltd, Glasgow.

PREFACE AND ACKNOWLEDGEMENTS

This volume describes the development of twelve villages which now form part of the City of Glasgow, south of the Clyde. Most of the communities grew up on lands granted by the Crown or by the High Steward to powerful families in Renfrewshire, and they became part of the City in comparatively recent times. Govan and Gorbals, however, were for long under the authority of the See of Glasgow.

The author gratefully acknowledges the assistance received from the staffs of the History and Glasgow Room of the Mitchell Library, Glasgow City Archives, Glasgow University Library, Glasgow University Archives, Paisley Library, the Scottish Record Office, and the Map Room of the National Library of Scotland. Thanks go also to the many individuals and societies who have supplied information, including Bellarmine Resource Centre, Govan Fair Association, and the Gorbals Regeneration Project.

The following have kindly given permission to quote from their works or to reproduce photographs:

Adam McNaughtan for *The Jeely Piece Song,* p. 71.

Harper Collins Publishers Limited for *The Letters of Edwin Lutyens to his Wife Lady Emily,* edited by Clayre Percy and Jane Ridley, 1985, p. 132.

Barrhead and Neilston Historical Association, p. 126.

Glasgow City Archives, pp. 67, 76.

Glasgow Museums, The People's Palace, p. 179.

Glasgow University Library, Department of Special Collections, p. 70.

Mitchell Library, Glasgow, pp. 6, 18, 40, 52, 83, 116, 131, 145, 167, 189.

The Scottish National Portrait Gallery, p. 26.

The Tron Theatre Company, p. 166.

Other photographs by R M Smart.

Glasgow, 1996, *Aileen Smart.*

CONTENTS

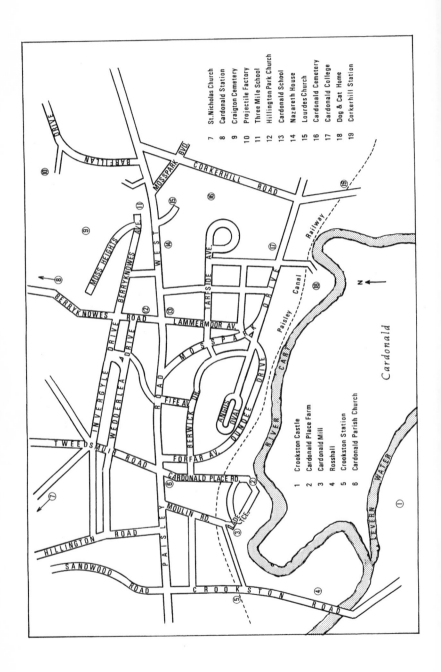

1 Crookston Castle
2 Cardonald Place Farm
3 Cardonald Mill
4 Rosshall
5 Crookston Station
6 Cardonald Parish Church

7 St. Nicholas Church
8 Cardonald Station
9 Craigton Cemetery
10 Projectile Factory
11 Three Mile School
12 Hillington Park Church
13 Cardonald School
14 Nazareth House
15 Lourdes Church
16 Cardonald Cemetery
17 Cardonald College
18 Dog & Cat Home
19 Corkerhill Station

Cardonald

CHAPTER 1

CARDONALD

The history of Cardonald begins at the end of the 15th century when the lands of Cardonald were granted to Sir Alan Stewart, a natural son of Sir John Stewart of Darnley. Sir John was owner of the mighty Crookston Castle nearby and was the ancestor of Henry Darnley, husband of Queen Mary. Around 1565 a descendant of Sir Alan built his own castle on the north bank of the river White Cart and called this the Palace, or 'Place' of Cardonald. Not long afterwards, in the reign of James Vl, the Cardonald lands passed by marriage to the Stewarts of Blantyre. By the end of the 18th century the lands had been subdivided into a number of smaller estates. Some of these, such as Rosshall and Craigton, remain substantially intact, although no longer as private estates. Others, along with the farmlands, now survive only in place-names like Hillington, Berryknowes and Mosspark.

In 1782 four small communities, 13 families in all, were reported living on the Cardonald estate: at the Place of Cardonald; at the milltown on the Cart; on the lands of Henderstone at the Three Mile House, where until recently a coal work had been carried on; and in the village of Cardonald where the great road from Glasgow to Paisley leads through at the four mile stone. Three Mile House village was later known as 'Halfway'. The 'great road' referred to is the present Paisley Road West, formed as a toll road in 1753. The present Halfway House Post Office near the corner of Mosspark Boulevard, and the Cardonald Post Office near Moulin Road, roughly correspond with the three mile and the four mile stones. The original road from Glasgow to Paisley took a route a little to the north. From the Halfway it passed in front of Moss Heights, crossed Berryknowes Road and followed the line of the lane between Wedderlea Drive and Invergyle Drive before dropping down past South Hillington farm to rejoin the present road near Barshaw Park. Both roads are marked on Thomas Richardson's *Plan of the Town of Glasgow and Country seven miles round* published in 1795. This map also shows the boundary between Govan and Abbey parishes crossing Paisley Road just west of Halfway House.

In the first decade of the 19th century the Glasgow, Paisley and Ardrossan Canal was led through Cardonald. Its purpose was to transport goods and passengers, and Cardonald escaped industrial development. The area only began to develop as a residential suburb after the opening of Cardonald Station in 1879 and Crookston Station in 1885. After the arrival of the electric tramcars in 1903, the growth of Cardonald began in earnest along the stretch of road between the little villages of Cardonald and Halfway. The first streets of terraced villas were formed at right angles to Paisley Road in the Tweedsmuir and Fife Avenue areas. Behind these, long streets of bungalows were built parallel to Paisley Road in the 1920s, and finally the high ground to north and south was filled by Corporation houses and Western Heritable flatted cottages after Cardonald became part of Glasgow in 1926. The high flats at Moss Heights were built in the early 1950s.

The earliest public building in Cardonald was the school erected at the corner of Lammermoor Avenue and Paisley Road in 1860. By 1910 most of Cardonald's other public buildings were in place: the parish church, police station and Nazareth House on the south side of Paisley Road, and the United Free Church (now Hillington Park Church of Scotland) at the top of Berryknowes Road. Since then the one mile stretch between Three Mile House and the four mile stone has been filled by shops, banks, cinemas, cafes, garages and a library, most of which have survived to form the heart of a community, which has successfully formed and retained its own identity and character.

Crookston Castle: 'a lofty but greatly shattered ruin'

Through Crookston Castle's lonely wa's
The wintry wind howls wild and dreary.

Crookston Castle surmounts a hill overlooking the Levern Water which flows into the river White Cart a little way downstream. Two castles have stood on the site. The first was a wooden castle probably built in the 12th century by Sir Robert de Croc of Neilston, who received the lands of Crookston from Walter fitz Alan, High Steward of Scotland. The impressive earthen ringwork which wholly surrounded this early castle still remains intact. It consists of a wide ditch and outer bank with a single entrance on the west side. A wooden palisade probably provided extra defence for the

A view from Hillington Park Circus over a variety of Cardonald housing towards Moss Heights. These were the first high flats in Glasgow, built in the early 1950s on the Craigton estate.

interior buildings, which are likely to have been entirely of timber.

In the 14th century Crookston came into the ownership of the Stewarts of Darnley, and in the early 15th century a stone castle was built within the defences. This is now the second oldest building in Glasgow after the Cathedral. Crookston is a massive tower-house of unique design. It consisted of a central keep with a large 24 feet high vaulted great hall on the first floor, built above a vaulted ground storey. A square tower projected at each of the four corners, but only the north-east tower has survived to full height. This tower contained the bed-chambers of the lord and his lady, and it is possible to climb the winding stair and a ladder to the roof to enjoy the extensive views northwards over Cardonald and far beyond the Clyde.

Crookston Castle is thought to have been built by the Sir John Stewart of Darnley who commanded a Scottish force in France during the Hundred Years War. For his part in securing a victory at Bauge for the Dauphin, later Charles VII of France, Sir John was created Comte d'Evreux and Seigneur d'Aubigny. He was killed in 1429 at the siege of Orleans and is buried in Orleans Cathedral. Sir John is still celebrated in France and has his own museum at

Aubigny-sur-Nere in the Loire valley. He married Elizabeth, daughter of the last Celtic Earl of Lennox, and their grandson, also Sir John, became the first Stewart Earl of Lennox in 1488. The first earl rose in rebellion against James IV and during the siege of Crookston Castle which followed, Mons Meg was dragged from Edinburgh to take part in the assault with devastating effect. 'A lofty but greatly shattered ruin' is as apt a description of the castle today as when the words were written in the 1860s.

According to legend, it was underneath a yew tree at Crookston that Queen Mary and Henry, Lord Darnley, plighted their troth. The tree was much celebrated in song and verse and became so mutilated by relic-hunters that its remains were taken in 1817 to Pollok where G Finlay, a craftsman from Cartcraigs at Pollokshaws, cut the wood into square pieces of about an eighth of an inch in size to resemble stones and created a perfect model of the castle. This model has stood for many years on the top landing of the staircase at Pollok House. Another tree, the 'Darnley Sycamore', has so far survived at the junction of Nitshill Road and Kennishead Road, about two miles south of Crookston. Mary and Darnley are supposed to have sat under this tree when she nursed him back to health after an illness.

The lands and castle of Crookston passed through many owners until they were finally purchased from the Duke of Montrose in 1757 by Sir John Maxwell of Nether Pollok, who repaired the castle and saved it from total ruin. In 1931 Sir John Stirling-Maxwell presented Crookston Castle to the National Trust for Scotland as its first property. The castle is now in the guardianship of Historic Scotland.

The Stewarts of Cardonald and the Place of Cardonald

The lands of Cardonald appear to have been in the possession of a Norral or Normanville family during the first part of the 15th century, when Johannes Norwald, 'dominus de Cardownalde' was witness to a legal document drawn up at Paisley in 1413. In 1487 the lands passed into the ownership of Alan Stewart, the natural son of Sir John Stewart of Darnley, the first Stewart Earl of Lennox. A descendant, James Stewart of Cardonald, is believed to have built a castle in 1565, known as the Palace or 'Place' of Cardonald. Cardonald Place farm now occupies the site.

James Stewart died in 1584 and is buried in Paisley Abbey. A

Crookston Castle was a stronghold of the Stewarts of Darnley. It was built in the early 15th century on the site of an earlier castle belonging to Sir Robert de Croc. Now in the care of Historic Scotland.

gravestone set in the wall bears a Latin inscription, surrounding the crest of the Darnley coat of arms. This reads in translation:

> Here lies an honorable man, James Stewart of Cardonald, sometime Captain of the Guard of Scotland to France and deceased on 14th day of January 1584.

After the death of James Stewart, Cardonald passed to his nephew, Walter Stewart, son of his sister Margaret and Sir John Stewart of Minto, provost of Glasgow. Walter Stewart was Commendator of Blantyre Priory, and had been a boyhood companion of King James VI, who created him Lord Blantyre in 1606.

The grand-daughter of the first Lord Blantyre was Frances Teresa Stewart, 'La Belle Stewart', who made a considerable impact on the court of Charles II and is thought to have been the model

Cardonald House in 1835 from a lithograph by David Allan. An idyllic view of the house built by James Stewart of Cardonald on the north bank of the White Cart river.

for Britannia on the British coinage. Pepys described her as 'the greatest beauty I ever saw in I think my life'. Frances married the Duke of Richmond and Lennox after declaring herself 'willing to marry any gentleman of £1,500 a year who would have her in honour'. The magnificent 17 piece silver-gilt toilet service on display in the National Museum of Scotland, known as the 'Lennoxlove Service' belonged to Frances and was possibly gifted by Charles II himself. The service was made in Paris over a period of 14 years and only four such sets survive. Lennoxlove House, the home of 'La Belle Stewart' is now the seat of the Duke of Hamilton.

In 1710 Crawfurd wrote of Cardonald in his *History of Renfrewshire*:

> Near to the castle of Crocston, upon the opposite side of the river, stands the place and lands of Cardonald, well planted and beautified with pleasant gardens; one of the seats of the Rt. Hon. Walter, Lord Blantyre.

Cardonald remained in the possession of the Stewarts of Blantyre for several generations. The family also purchased the Erskine estate and the 12th and last Lord Blantyre died in Erskine House in 1900. The estates then passed to the family of Laird of Erskine and Lennoxlove, owners of the Wedderlea estate in East Lothian. Many street names in Cardonald have names associated with the Lothians and the Borders: Lammermoor, Oxton, Swinton, Selkirk and others.

When Hugh MacDonald visited Cardonald in 1851 on one of his *Rambles* he reported that the 'picturesque castle of Cardonald' had been demolished 'within these few years' and a neat, modern farm-steading erected on the site. In 1975 the farmstead was converted by the Glasgow Parks Department into a house, now called Cardonald Place Farm. The present house has the date 1848, and a stone inserted over the front entrance has a coat of arms with the letters I (or J) S, the motto Toujours Avant (always first) and the date 1565. The coat of arms shows the Stewart checks, the French fleur de lys and the four roses of the Celtic earls of Lennox. This is not an officially recognised coat of arms, but is likely to have been adopted by the James Stewart of Cardonald presumed to have built the 'Place' in 1565, or by his brother-in-law, Sir John Stewart of Minto.

The Glasgow, Paisley and Johnstone Canal

Work began on the Glasgow, Paisley and Ardrossan Canal in 1807. The canal was promoted mainly by the Earl of Eglinton, and its purpose included the export of Scottish coal to Ireland and the import of Irish grain through the proposed new harbour at Ardrossan. An eleven mile stretch of canal between Port Eglinton in Glasgow and a basin at Johnstone was opened in 1811, but funds ran out and the canal proceeded no further. From Port Eglinton the canal ran via Dumbreck to the north bank of the White Cart at Cardonald, where there was a small quay at Rosshall. The canal crossed the Cart by an aqueduct at Blackhall before reaching Paisley and continued through two tunnels to its terminus at Johnstone. A proposed branch canal to Hurlet was never built, but Rosshall quay was used to load minerals and stone drawn by horses along a wooden waggonway from the coalworks at Hurlet and the quarries at Nitshill.

In the 1830s the canal was particularly successful in attracting passenger transport. At first the Canal Company had to compete with steam carriages operating from George Square in Glasgow to

A passenger at Crookston station awaits the arrival of the train from Glasgow Central to Paisley Canal. The Canal Line was reopened in 1989, and the station buildings are now private houses.

the Tontine Hotel in Paisley, but an accident at the Three Mile House led to a ban on their use in Scotland. On Tuesday 26 July 1834, the two o'clock carriage from Glasgow stopped at the top of the hill outside the Three Mile House to take on fuel and water. It had just restarted its journey when one of the right-hand wheels gave way, and as the machine fell, the boiler was crushed, causing the vehicle to explode. Five persons died from their injuries, and several of the other twelve passengers suffered severe fractures and scaldings. A woman passer-by was also badly scalded.

Much of the success of the canal was due to William Houston of Johnstone Castle who introduced swift passenger boats designed to race like gig boats, which a single horse could pull at twelve miles per hour. There were no locks on the canal, but plenty of corners and bends, and it was strictly forbidden to run at speed in the narrow part at Dumbreck unless there were few passengers. In 1839 the company carried over 400,000 passengers, twice as many as the Forth & Clyde canal, and in 1840 there were 13 boats daily between Glasgow and Paisley from which passengers could enjoy the romantic views of Crookston Castle and the unspoiled countryside. At one time the company employed 78 horses, many of which were well-known to the local residents.

Among the favourites were Moses, England, Sadler, Gypsy, Doctor, Rob Roy, Solomon and Smiler. Great concern was shown by the company for the welfare of its horses, and a separate shed was provided at Paisley Basin for sick horses.

By the 1830s the shadow of railway competition was starting to fall over the canal. The Glasgow and Paisley Joint Railway was opened in 1840 and three years later the canal company agreed to give up carrying passengers and parcels in return for an annual payment of £1,367. The canal company continued to carry freight and survived until 1869 when it was bought by the Glasgow and South Western Railway Company. The canal itself lasted until 1881 when it was filled in and laid as a railway which opened in 1885 as the Paisley Canal line with a station at Crookston. The canal line was closed to traffic in 1982, but reopened as a single line in 1989. Crookston Station was partially destroyed by fire during the period of closure, but has now been restored as a private house.

Cardonald Mills

On 28 May 1816 John Snodgrass, who had previously farmed at Inchinnan, took possession of the Mill of Cardonald which Lord Blantyre had leased to him for a period of 19 years. The lease also gave Snodgrass the occupancy of 'the commodious mansion of Cardonald', the old home of the Stewarts of Cardonald, and an ideal residence on the banks of the Cart for John, his wife Agnes Millar, and their eight children. Snodgrass began by engaging four employees: William Purdon carter, at a wage of 14s 6d per week; Robert Steven miller, 18s; James Stewart engineer, 13s; and Alan McLean orra man 10s. After some delay due to negotiations with the canal company over water supply, John Snodgrass wrote in his log book on 16 July 1816: 'This day I began to work, having the mill repaired and things put in order'. Snodgrass had recognised the advantages of a mill close to the newly opened canal, enabling him to easily despatch his produce, mainly peasemeal and oatmeal, to the provision merchants of Glasgow and Paisley.

After the death of John Snodgrass in 1837, his eldest son, James, who had spent some time at sea, took over the mill. The second son, John, had three years previously entered the Glasgow office of John McColl & Co, an old established firm of grain merchants. In 1851 the two brothers formed a partnership as millers and grain merchants, but the partnership only lasted three years. John then went into business in Glasgow with a third brother, Robert, as the firm of J & R Snodgrass, with a mill at Port Dundas where they could import grain from the Baltic via the Forth & Clyde canal. In 1861 J & R Snodgrass acquired the Washington Mills in Anderston and became one of the largest millers and flour merchants in Glasgow. The business is now part of Allied Mills, and the name of J & R Snodgrass stands in bold letters on the flour mill on the Broomielaw just to the east of the Kingston Bridge.

James Snodgrass continued to live at Cardonald, and lived in Cardonald Place farm which was built with stone from the old Place of Cardonald after it was demolished in 1848. About the same time an older farmstead on the old road from Glasgow to Paisley, shown on Richardson's map as Cardonneltown, was renamed Hillhead farm. This was probably the original farmhouse of the estate and stood near the intersection of Wedderlea Drive with Tweedsmuir Road. The old armorial stone with the initials of James Stewart of Cardonald was transferred from Cardonald castle to the new farm-stead, and by good luck the initials coincided with those of the new owner. James Snodgrass continued to play a leading role in the community, and it was largely due to his exertions that Cardonald Subscription School was kept going at Three Mile House and was replaced by a new school on Paisley Road in 1860. Cardonald Mill was also rebuilt in 1848 and remained in use until 1958 when it was demolished along with a number of adjoining cottages and replaced by the houses in Lade Terrace.

Cardonald School

Cardonald School has occupied three different sites during its long existence which is believed to have begun as far back as 1790 when a blacksmith was reported teaching a class of children in the village of Three Mile House. This school was put on a subscription basis in 1826. In 1860 a new school and teacher's house were erected at the corner of Paisley Road and Lammermoor Avenue. This school is now used as a Careers Office. Cardonald Primary School was transferred from this building in 1966 to its present site in Angus Oval.

A number of old documents recovered from beneath the foundation stone of the school in Paisley Road West give a valuable insight into the operation of Three Mile Subscription School between 1841 and 1860. Over these twenty years the name of

James Snodgrass of Cardonald Mills regularly heads the list of subscribers. Contributions were also made by the local farmers and tradesmen. In 1855, 15 subscribers gave from £2 to 2s 6d each, a total of just over £13. This sum paid the teacher's annual salary of £9 3s 4d, the school rent £2 12s 6d, coals £1 3s 6d and cleaning 3s 8d. Want of funds frequently made it impossible to induce any teacher to accept the situation. The office bearers in 1855 were: Preses James Snodgrass; Treasurer James Arneil land steward; Committee of Management James McGie of Berryknowes farm, William Lyon of Hillhead farm, Robert Harvie smith and farrier and Daniel Russell master wright. This early school is shown on the Ordnance Survey map of 1859 as a small building near the east end of the present Moss Heights, just within the Govan parish portion of Three Mile House village.

In 1860 James Richardson of Ralston House, a tea and sugar merchant in Glasgow, left a legacy of £1,000 'to assist in erecting and maintaining a school in the neighbourhood of the Three Mile House'. Lord Blantyre gave the site and a gift of money, the tenant farmers gave free cartage of building stone, and on 6 September 1860 the foundation stone of the new school was laid by James Snodgrass. The teacher was now William Harkness and the list of scholars he prepared in 1860 is still extant. It lists by name 30 scholars living in Three Mile House and 28 others at the farms of North Henderston, East Henderston, Ibroxhill, Hillington, Crookston, Berryknowe and Ibrox, and at Hillington Toll, Cardonald Smithy, Moss Station and Craigton Nursery. The subjects taught were English reading, arithmetic, grammar and geography.

After 1865 the admission register uses the name Halfway House instead of Three Mile House for the village. Until 1883 the fathers' occupations are given: mostly miners or agricultural workers such as ploughman, farmer, dairyman, gardener, shepherd, as well as a few tradesmen and a policeman. There are increasing numbers of children of railwaymen, in particular from the railway village of Corkerhill, which later had its own infant school, run as an annexe of Cardonald.

By the 1890s the school was seriously overcrowded and an extension was opened in November 1899. The log book reports that work during the building operations was 'at all times trying to the Patience' especially when the only entrance to the school was on planks laid across the drain, but 'the scholars are very careful and put up with the privations wonderfully well'. By 1901 the roll had risen to 208 and in 1911 the school was again extended to accommodate all the 344 pupils on the roll. Class sizes could now be reduced to not more than 50.

Alexander Lochhead became headmaster in 1908 and took charge of the 'Supplementary Classes' for older pupils who had not gone on to a secondary school. Each of these pupils was given a plot in the headmaster's garden and had to keep records of the growth of plants for nature study. Between May 1909 and February 1910 Mr Lochhead led his pupils on visits to Edinburgh and Stirling; for a sail down the Clyde to see the shipping and to get on board the battleship *Caesar* at Dunoon; to the St Andrew's Halls to hear Sir E H Shackleton's lecture on *Nearest the South Pole;* and to see the launch of the *Parramata* at Govan. All pupils of the four next highest classes had also been taken by Mr Lochhead (one class at a time) to visit the Glasgow Museum. Many later outings were made to Millport Marine Station.

In 1954 Angus Oval Annexe was opened for the pupils of Cardonald Junior Secondary School, and after a further reorganisation of education, Cardonald Primary School removed to Angus Oval where there was now accommodation for 500 pupils in twelve classrooms. The opening ceremony took place on 10 February 1966 when an assembly of parents and friends were entertained by the school choir who sang *In Praise of Islay* and *The Uist Tramping Song*. The vote of thanks was given by the head teacher, Mrs W W Houston MA.

Alexander Lochhead was also scoutmaster of the local troop for twelve years from 1916. The troop was formed in 1909 as the 30th Glasgow (1st Cardonald) Scout Troop and had their own wooden hut on an open site between Wedderlea Drive and Hillington Park Circus. The Wolf Cubs were started in 1917 and the Rover Scouts in 1921. Five years later the troop built new premises which consisted of a central hall flanked by four old railway carriages, two on either side, which served as patrol and scouters' dens. The hall was destroyed by vandalism in 1974, after which a new hall was built in Lammermoor Avenue and opened by Bruce Millan, then Secretary of State for Scotland.

Other local primary schools are Hillington, which like Cardonald is perched on top of a drumlin, Sandwood, Lourdes and Our Lady of the Rosary. Lourdes Secondary School in Kirriemuir

School's Out! Pupils of Our Lady of the Rosary Primary School dash for home after another hard day in the classroom.

Avenue was opened in 1957. Cardonald College offers a range of full-time courses leading to SCOTVEC and other qualifications in a variety of subjects including industrial design, graphic design, information technology, building studies and travel and tourism. The College opened in 1972 and now has 1,800 students in full-time courses and another 3,000 in part-time and leisure classes.

Cardonald Churches

Following a meeting in Cardonald School in 1887, a congregation was formed and a church built with the assistance of money gifted by the local landowners, Lord Blantyre, Sir Charles Cayzer of Ralston and James Cowan of Rosshall. The following year the church became Cardonald Parish Church with the Rev William Liston as first minister. The site was on the corner of Cardonald Place Road and Paisley Road, at the centre of the original village of Cardonald. The design of the church was based on Corrie Church in Arran, but this proved too small for the growing population and a west aisle was added in 1899 and an east aisle in 1925. The accommodation was again increased by halls built in 1940 and linking rooms added in 1960.

13

The two other Church of Scotland congregations in Cardonald are Hillington Park and St Nicholas. Hillington Park was begun as a Church Extension charge by the United Free church in 1908. Services were held in a hall-church until a new church was erected in 1925. St Nicholas Parish Church in Harlaw Crescent also began as an extension charge in 1937, built by the Baird Trustees.

The first services for Catholics in Cardonald were held in Maryland House, an early 18th century estate house owned by the Rowans of Govan and latterly by the Stevens of Bellahouston. The house, which stands on the west of Corkerhill Road near Paisley Road, has been restored and is now a private social club. Maryland was bought by the Archdiocese of Glasgow in 1902 and used as a convent by the Sisters of Nazareth until Nazareth House was built four years later as a convent and home for the aged poor and destitute children. Services were then held in the chapel in Nazareth House until Our Lady of Lourdes Church was opened in Lourdes Avenue in 1939.

In 1873 much of the Craigton estate became the Govan Burgh Cemetery. As Craigton Cemetery, it is now a private burial ground. The Glasgow District Council is responsible for Cardonald Cemetery which was opened in 1922. There is a small Jewish cemetery within the grounds and an interesting group of war graves from the Second World War, including the resting places of British naval personnel and Polish and German soldiers.

Rosshall House and Gardens

To the south of Cardonald Mill, and surrounded on three sides by the river Cart, is the estate of Rosshall, which takes its name from the Ross family of Hawkhead who originally owned the lands. Rosshall was acquired in the late 18th century by Peter Murdoch, a Glasgow merchant, who laid out the grounds, planting trees and creating 'several straight and serpentine green walks'. A little winding rivulet played over a cascade into the river, and opposite where the Levern Water joins the Cart, 30 acres of grounds were made into an orchard. The avenue of lime trees near the river may have been planted at this time.

In the 1870s the estate was purchased by James Cowan, a Barrhead man and head of the firm of Messrs Cowan & Co, carriers and contractors to several Scottish and English railway companies and to shipping companies in Glasgow. James Cowan built the

Rosshall House was built by James Cowan in 1877 and later became the home of the Lobnitz family. Part of the grounds are Rosshall Park, open to the public. The house is now a private hospital.

baronial style Rosshall House in 1877, and occupied it until his death in 1907, aged 80 years. The landscaping firm of Pullman & Son was commissioned to reconstruct, regardless of expense, the estate gardens. The result was the appearance of a new artificial lake and a new course for Murdoch's little rivulet over waterfalls and through grottos and rock gardens. Part of the estate is now Rosshall Park, opened to the public by Glasgow Corporation in 1965. A walkway from the gardens leads along the banks of the Cart and is linked by foot-bridges to Cardonald and to the Pollok housing estate.

Like many of his contemporaries, James Cowan was a connoisseur of the arts and Rosshall House was designed to display his rich collection of silver, jewellery, porcelain, books and paintings.

Some of these were housed in the gallery above the hall, reached by a staircase lit by stained glass windows representing the Arts. The sale of the Rosshall collection following Cowan's death took place on seven days over a period of two weeks in February 1908. The contents of the wine cellar were sold on the first day and included 400 bottles of wine, port and sherry, two casks containing 35 gallons of whisky, small quantities of brandy and rum and one bottle of gin. Also sold on the same day was his President's Gold Badge of the Cronies Club, a dining club in Glasgow, which held 'first rate musical evenings' and of which Cowan had long been a member. Among the coins sold were a silver ryall, a two-thirds ryall, and a one-third ryall of 1565, sometimes called the Crookston Dollar, minted to commemorate the marriage of Queen Mary with Darnley. Among Cowan's personal effects were three travelling rugs made of bearskin, fine sable, and tiger cat skin, as well as a skin foot muff. Several of the 'articles of vertu' sold the following day had come from the Hamilton House collection. The sale of the 1469 books took place over four days. Works included books on Glasgow and Paisley, the *Steamboat Companion 1825* and *Lumsden's Guide to Loch Lomond and Loch Ketturin 1831* along with such treasures as a *Nuremberg Chronicle* of 1493 printed by hand and illustrated with woodcuts, bound in calf, tooled and gilt. Among the 205 oil paintings, water colours and etchings were works by Rembrandt, van Dyck, Romney, Constable, Turner, Landseer, Thomas Faed and Sam Bough.

James Cowan was a bachelor and left money to several hospitals and £10,000 for the purchase of land for a public hall and park in Barrhead to be called the 'Cowan Park'. His staff were rewarded for their long service: a life annuity of £100 to James McFarland, his butler and house steward; £10 for each year of service to Archibald MacKay the head coachman, Robert Pringle the head gardener, and Maggie McLeod housemaid; and £5 for each year of service to the domestic servants, under-gardeners and outdoor labourers.

The next owner of Rosshall was Frederick Lobnitz, head of a ship-building firm owned by his father Henry, who had come from Denmark to work on Clydeside in the 1850s. Lobnitz & Co specialised in building dredgers and rock cutting machinery for a world-wide market and built more than 100 vessels for the Suez Canal contractors. Frederick spent several months directing submarine rock excavations on the Suez Canal before entering into partnership with his father in 1888. In 1919 Frederick Lobnitz was knighted for his wartime services as Deputy Director of Munitions for Scotland under William Weir. After his death in 1930 the firm continued under family control until taken over by Weirs in 1959.

In 1948 the Rosshall estate was acquired by Glasgow Corporation who leased the house to the Glasgow and West of Scotland Commercial College for use as a hotel school which later became part of Strathclyde University. In 1982 the house was purchased for use as Scotland's first wholly commercial private hospital.

From shells to tractors to steel houses

In 1917 production of shells was transferred from the works of G & J Weir at Cathcart to a new factory at Cardonald, known as the National Projectile Factory. During the war William Weir was Minister of Munitions and his Deputy was Frederick Lobnitz of Rosshall House. The new factory was situated on a 24 acre site on part of the former Craigton estate, between Barfillan Drive and the railway where excellent communications could be effected with the various docks on the south bank of the Clyde. One of the features of the factory was the creche provided for the children of the war widows who worked in the factory.

After the war the site and all the buildings including railway sidings, and all power, lighting and heating plant was sold for £170,000 to Wallace Farm Implements Ltd. The product manufactured by this firm at Cardonald was the 'Glasgow' tractor, Scotland's only native tractor. The Scottish Agricultural Museum at Ingleston has one of these Glasgow tractors on display. This was a machine noted for its stability and its capacity for working in wet weather. It was designed with two wheels at the front and one at the rear, all power driven. The three wheels were positively driven when the vehicle was travelling straight, while the rear wheel and one wheel only were positively driven when the vehicle was negotiating a curve. This meant that the load would remain under all conditions equally distributed on all three wheels for maximum weight and power. The tractor had wide sales initially to parts of the Empire and Europe. It was popular in Spain where it could deal with muddy waterlogged rice fields. But the machine was not sold in great quantity and competition from the American Fordson tractor which retailed at £120, less than one third of the

Well wrapped up against the snow. These youngsters are attending the creche for the children of war widows working in the National Projectile Factory set up at Cardonald in 1917.

price of the Glasgow tractor, brought about the closure of the Cardonald factory in 1924.

The site was then used by Lord Weir to manufacture pre-fabricated housing, following a request from the government for suggestions to help the national housing situation after the war. Weir considered that concrete involved too much labour on site, all steel was too costly, and chose a composite design involving a timber frame and steel sheeting. An experimental bungalow was made at Cathcart by skilled men, but the firm agreed to carry the scheme further only on condition that development work was removed entirely from the engineering works at Cathcart. The first contract was started at Newton Stewart in March 1925 and by December the same year 200 houses had been completed on 48 different sites from Kirkwall to Plymouth. The majority of orders were for ten to fifteen houses in one place, the exceptions being the Middle Ward of Lanarkshire and Linlithgow with 100 houses each, and Robroyston where 40 were erected. The average cost of a house was £400 and six to eight men could finish a house ready for occupation in six days. A glowing testimonial was received in June 1926 from Dr Harper, the Medical Officer of Health for Stranraer, who wrote that the steel houses were doing splendid, during the cold winter months they were the best heated houses in the town, and to treat a sick person in they were first class.

Faced with possible opposition from building trade workers, local authorities were reluctant to erect Weir housing. A government inquiry failed to find a solution, and the factory was vacated in March 1928. Nevertheless, about 3,000 Weir steel houses were produced at Cardonald and erected, mainly in Scotland. A pair of prefabricated 'Eastwood' semi-detached steel cottages remain near the entrance to the factory in Barfillan Drive. The site of the factory is now occupied by allotments and various industrial firms, including Howden Buffalo, manufacturers of air compressors.

Cinemas, theatres and cats and dogs

The earliest of Cardonald's three cinemas was the Mosspark, which was situated on Paisley Road opposite Barfillan Drive, and opened by Caledonian Associated Cinemas in 1924. The 'Mossie' was a plain building but enjoyed a loyal following, and survived until 1975 when it was demolished to make way for a Department of Social Security Office. The two other cinemas were built by George Singleton: the Westway in 1934, and the Aldwych, later known as the Vogue, in 1938. The Westway closed as a cinema in 1960, became the Flamingo Ballroom, and since 1966 has been a Bingo Hall. The Aldwych seated 2,500, twice as many as the Westway, but was the first to close in 1964 and Safeways now occupies the site. The name lives on in the Aldwych Special Pizzas and the delectable Aldwych Gelato Sundaes on offer with the cones, single and double nougats, sponges and oysters in the cafe of the same name across the road.

Cardonald never had its own theatre as such, but it could boast a temple of drama, erected in the grounds of Craigton House by Annette Hutchison, the Edinburgh-born widow of a merchant who had bought the Craigton estate in the 1850s, and who had 'a craze for theatricals'. The theatre was described as a building of goodly proportions and well situated for its purpose. Here Annette entertained her guests at considerable expense with the assistance of a staff comprising a footman, serving maid, cook, housemaid, under housemaid and scullery maid.

After Mrs Hutchison left Craigton for Paisley, the mansion house was let and while in the occupancy of James Spencer, a ship-owner, it was destroyed by fire. The offices and stables were then let as a house for cats and dogs, according to one contemporary commentator, 'a very laudable purpose certainly, but not in keeping with the traditions for which they were erected'. Fortunately new premises were found for the animals, and the West of Scotland Dog and Cat Home was opened by Lady Hersey Baird of Erskine in May 1909, on ground later acquired by Glasgow Corporation on the site of Mid Henderston farm. The buildings consisted of four groups: general offices and keepers' houses at the gateway; eight houses for cats; dog-kennels for 50 stray dogs and 49 for boarders; and a chamber where the animals were destroyed by anaesthesia. In 1994 a £1.2 million extension was added to the home. The Glasgow Dog and Cat Home has now merged with the SSPCA to provide a network of animal care covering the West of Scotland. There is accommodation at Cardonald for about 200 dogs and 30 cats, of which 95 per cent are strays. Facilities are being extended to include other stray domestic pets such as rabbits, gerbils and even the odd stray snake.

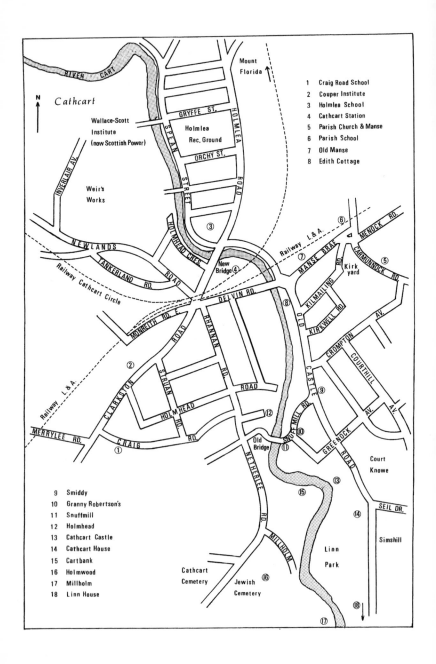

Cathcart

N

1   Craig Road School
2   Couper Institute
3   Holmlea School
4   Cathcart Station
5   Parish Church & Manse
6   Parish School
7   Old Manse
8   Edith Cottage

9   Smiddy
10   Granny Robertson's
11   Snuffmill
12   Holmhead
13   Cathcart Castle
14   Cathcart House
15   Cartbank
16   Holmwood
17   Millholm
18   Linn House

CHAPTER 2
CATHCART

O, scenes of my childhood and dear to my heart,
The green waving woods on the margin of Cart,
How oft in the morning of life I have strayed
By the stream of the vale and the grass covered glade.

The village of Cathcart grew up on the right bank of the river White Cart below the crag on which the Cathcart family, first heard of in Renfrewshire in the 12th century, built their castle, sadly demolished in 1980. A suggested derivation for the name is from the British 'caer' meaning 'fort' and the name of the river. This was also the place where a main route from Glasgow to Ayrshire crossed the Cart by ford and later by stone bridge. The parish church of Cathcart was donated to the monastery of Paisley around 1179 and stood at the heart of an extensive parish which stretched from Polmadie in the north to Williamwood in the south.

The area developed in the 18th century as the waters of Cart were exploited by mill-owners producing paper and snuff and by the proprietors of bleach and printfields. However, when a new bridge was built half a mile downriver in 1800, the old village was by-passed and declined in importance and population, although it increasingly attracted city ramblers, artists and poets like Thomas Campbell who wrote of the scenes of his childhood on the margin of Cart. At the same time a new village, New Cathcart, grew up along the Busby road, now Clarkston Road, which was opened in 1810.

After the arrival of the railway in 1886, Cathcart became a popular residential suburb for city workers. There followed the building of churches, schools, a public hall and library, and within two decades tenements lined the streets and fine villas covered the former farmlands of Newlands and Merrylee on the western fringes of Cathcart.

Cathcart remained independent from Glasgow until 1912. The inter-war years saw large areas of house-building in the King's Park area to the east and the circle was completed by the development of Simshill on the Castle Mains farm in the 1950s. The principal employers in Cathcart today are the engineering giant, Weir Pumps, and Scottish Power.

The Cathcart Family: 'courteous and fair, and of good fame'

The history of Cathcart begins in the 12th century when a Breton called Rainald held the lands of Cathcart in Renfrewshire and his successors took the name of the place. During the Wars of Independence Alan of Cathcart was a noted supporter of Robert I. One story has it that he was one of the knights who accompanied Douglas to the Crusades, and rescued the casket containing Bruce's heart from the fallen Douglas during the battle with the Moors in Spain. Barbour, in his heroic poem *The Brus* wrote of this very parfait gentle knight as:

> Worthy and wight
> stalwart and stout
> courteous and fair
> and of good fame

The successful return of Sir Alan is commemorated by the Cathcart Pillar in the nave of Paisley Abbey and a window depicting deeds of heroism.

By the middle of the 14th century the Cathcart family had acquired large estates in central Ayrshire. They still held intact the ancestral lands in Renfrewshire, and around 1452 the lands of Cathcart, Talgart (Tankerland) and Bogton were erected into a Barony by James II for Sir Alan Cathcart. From its style it seems likely that Cathcart Castle was built around this time. Plans show the keep as a simple rectangular structure about 50 feet by 30 feet, with a vaulted ground floor and four upper floors reached by an internal circular stair. The keep was surrounded, at a distance of ten feet, with curtain walls strengthened with round corners.

Between 1500 and 1535 there are numerous references to a debt to the crown, and the Cathcart lands in Renfrewshire were broken up, the largest part passing to the Semple family and later to John Maxwell of Williamwood and his cousin, John Maxwell of Blawarthill, the future owner of Nether Pollok. The castle appears to have remained inhabited until about 1740 when the materials were sold to a contractor who unroofed the castle 'intending to demolish the whole structure, and only desisted when he found it would not be remunerative to do so'. James Hill, a Glasgow lawyer, bought the portion of the estate containing the castle some 40

Cathcart Castle was the old seat of the Earls of Cathcart. The servants' cottages were demolished in the 1930s and the remains of the castle razed in 1980.

years later, but chose to build a new mansion a little east of the castle. This is sometimes referred to as Cartside House, but more often as Cathcart House. The house stood within the Linn Park, about 100 yards from the present entrance in Old Castle Road, opposite what is now Seil Drive.

The Cathcart family fortunes revived during the 18th century. The 8th Lord Cathcart fought for the government at Sheriffmuir and during the '45 his successor was ADC to Cumberland. The 10th Lord Cathcart bought back the ancestral lands from the representatives of James Hill in 1801, and in 1814 he received an earldom with the title Earl Cathcart and Baron Greenock. Earl Cathcart was ambassador to the Russian Court at St Petersburg from 1812 to 1821. His diplomatic services earned him many high Russian decorations. He was granted the freedom of the city of Glasgow 'in recognition of his military talents and virtues as a nobleman'. Lord Cathcart used Cathcart House as a residence and is recorded as living there in 1841, aged 85, with his Countess, his daughters the Ladies Louisa, Mary Elizabeth and Augustus, and ten

This engraving of Charles, 8th Baron Cathcart, is from a portrait by Allan Ramsay in the collections of the Scottish National Portrait Gallery. The 8th Baron fought for the Government at Sheriffmuir.

servants. He died two years later and his tomb in the Cathcart Aisle in Paisley Abbey is inscribed with his name, William Schaw Cathcart, and the family motto, 'I hope to speed'. A full length portrait of the Earl's sister, the beautiful Mary Cathcart, the Hon Mrs Graham, painted by Gainsborough when she was 18 years old, hangs in the National Gallery in Edinburgh.

Charles, the second Earl, became Governor General of Canada. His brother was General Sir George Cathcart, killed at the battle of Inkerman and buried on the heights above Sebastopol, known as Cathcart Hill. The sixth Earl, Alan Cathcart, present holder of the title, is a retired brigadier, who commanded the 152nd Highland Brigade from 1965 to 1966. His son and heir is Alan Andrew

Cathcart, Lord Greenock.

From the 1850s a succession of manufacturers and merchants occupied Cathcart House until Glasgow Corporation bought the estate to form part of the Linn Park and demolished the house in 1927. Demolition of the remains of the centuries-old A listed Cathcart Castle took place without warning on 1st September 1980. Until that date the castle survived to second floor level, with sections of the third remaining. Some parts of the curtain wall also survived on the south. The Corporation considered that the remains posed a safety hazard and the entire walls were reduced to three feet.

Across Old Castle Road from the castle is the detached part of the Linn Park known as the Court Knowe. Queen Mary is traditionally believed to have watched the battle of Langside from this hill, although at the time the castle belonged to Lord Semple, who along with Alan, the 4th Lord Cathcart, fought against the Queen. After leaving the scene Mary is supposed to have ridden towards Rutherglen by Mals Mire Road, now Menock Road. Mary's viewpoint has been marked successively by a hawthorn bush, a replacement thorn planted by James Hill, a clump of trees, a rough stone slab erected by General Sir George Cathcart and carved by his own hand with the Scottish Crown and 'M.R. 1568'. His nephew, the 3rd Earl, replaced this stone by the present granite slab with the crown, monogram of Mary R and the date.

The Kirktown of Cathcart: a considerable country village

Secure beneath its castle the village of Cathcart took shape. There was a meal mill on the river below the castle and a church about half a mile to the north-east near a holy well dedicated to St Oswald. The site chosen by the Cathcarts also gave them control of the important route from Glasgow to Ayr where it crossed the Cart by ford and later by bridge, and the village grew up along this route between kirk and river. The medieval layout has survived the centuries and can be retraced today by walking from the present church in Carmunnock Road past the old kirkyard, down Kilmailing Road, along Old Castle Road to the smiddy, now a restaurant, and along Snuffmill Road to the mill at the bridge.

Opinions vary about the date when Cathcart Old Bridge was built. Built into the eastern end of the north wall of the bridge about a foot from the top is a datestone 1624, and both the

Cathcart Bridge from William Simpson's Glasgow in the Forties. *The main route from Glasgow to Ayr crossed the White Cart by this two arched bridge. Nearby was Granny Robertson's inn, 'the wee thack house in the glen'. The chimney belongs to the mill which produced both paper and snuff last century.*

Glasgow Kirk Session records in 1622 and the Burgh Records in 1623 speak of raising money for building 'the brig of Cathcart'. A stone bridge with two arches is mentioned by both Crawfurd in 1710 and Semple in 1782. Some recent commentators, however, favour a date in the late 18th century for the bridge, or argue for an 18th-century reconstruction with the datestone a reinsertion. A well-known water-colour by the artist William Simpson, painted around 1845, shows the two arched bridge very much as it appears today, although surrounded by different buildings.

Glasgow Town Council was careful to keep this important route in good repair. There are several references throughout the 18th century to repairs on 'the way that leadeth to Cathcart'. In 1725 James Muir, mason, was paid for work at Cathcart Loan Bridge, and three years later John and Thomas McFies were given a contract to maintain 'the cawssey from Gorbals to Cathcart bridge stone below Robert Raes new house'. Richardson's map of 1795 shows the route of the old Glasgow to Ayr road very clearly — from Glasgow to Cathcart by way of Gorbals, Crosshill, the farms of Clincart and Mains of Cathcart, then through the Village and across the river by the old bridge, climbing up past Holmhead

The old Smiddy belonged to the Peddie family and is now a restaurant. It once had an outside stair to the upper storey which was used as a Dog Infirmary. The shop at the corner of the high tenement was a public house before becoming Kirkwood's Bakery.

House, then southwards through Braehead towards Netherlee, Mearns and Kilmarnock.

The Kirk Session records of Cathcart survive from 1701 and show a parish caring for its poor, its sick and the education of its children. Fines for breaches of moral discipline helped to fund the other services. One shilling was paid out in 1762 'to soaling and top-peicing Eliz. Youngs eldest boys shoes', 2s 6d in 1769 'to Hugh Mcfarland a poor man who has got his leg broken' and four pounds in 1782 'to the doctors for cutting off Robert Weir's leg and healing it'. The poors fund received an unexpected boost when James Hill, the Glasgow solicitor who bought Cathcart Castle and its policies, diverted into it the fines imposed on smugglers. Nevertheless, charity had to begin at home. Semple observed that 'No beggars, asking charity, are allowed to travel through this parish; being the same custom as at Eaglesham', and observing that as the idle wasp sucks the honey from the flower, to the injury of the industrious bee, so beggars suck the alms from simple people and prevent the really necessitous from having their wants relieved.

By 1782, according to Semple, Cathcart was a considerable village, containing about 36 houses, with a toll at the west end.

> The river White Cart runs through the village, where is a corn and wheat mill, the property of Sir James Maxwell of Nether-Pollock, being a few yards from the south side of the stone bridge with two arches above mentioned by Mr Craufurd, which is still standing. A little to the southward is a snuff mill, property of Mr James Hall, snuffmaker.

The corn and wheat mill referred to was long in the possession of the Hall family, evidently a family of note because 2s 6d was paid for 'Ringin the Bell' at James Hall's interment in 1763. The snuff mill was Millholm, begun as a paper mill by Nicholas Deschamp, a Frenchman, early in the 18th century and discussed below. Great quantities of wheat and potatoes were raised in the parish, particularly on the banks of the Cart, where about 20 acres of potatoes grew within a quarter mile of the church. Milk was also sent to Glasgow, and in the summer butter-milk, which provided 'a cheap and wholesome beverage to the lower classes of inhabitants of that great and populous city'.

With the turn of the century, however, the considerable Village of Cathcart was to suffer a sharp decline in population and importance. The reason was the building of Cathcart New Bridge in 1800.

Old Cathcart and New Cathcart

In 1800 Cathcart New Bridge, locally known as the Hunchback Bridge, was erected half a mile downstream from Old Cathcart. A new road was formed, Cathcart village was by-passed, church, manse and school fell into decay, and the considerable country village dwindled down to six or eight families, and Old Cathcart became a rural backwater. The new roadway was Clarkston Road, then known as the Busby road, opened in 1810, and the houses appearing along the wayside were the beginnings of New Cathcart. In the 1850s New Cathcart was still 'a quiet little village situated on both sides of the road leading from Glasgow to Busby' with a post office kept by the Inspector of Poor and a school 'well taught and well attended'. By 1881 the population had risen to 1656, mostly workers in the paper mills and at the printworks at Nether-lee, while the population of Old Cathcart had reached only 621.

As the century wore on the old village began to attract more and more summer visitors from Glasgow. These included poets, artists and ramblers like the indefatigable Hugh MacDonald who, on a visit in 1851, wrote admiringly of Cathcart with its score or so of houses with little patches of garden ground attached:

> Among these are a handsome farm-steading, a smithy or cartwright establishment, a snuff-mill, and in the neighbourhood an extensive paper manufactory. It has two public-houses, one of which, that of Mr Mitchell, is an exceedingly neat and comfortable little place of rest and refreshment...a favourite haunt of ramblers from the city, who with 'all the comforts of the Sautmarket' find besides the charms of rural beauty and quietude in its leafy bowers.

The second public-house, which did not merit further comment by MacDonald, was managed by the Warnock family. It later became the celebrated 'Wee Thatched Hoose in the Glen' where Jane Robertson presided until the hostelry was demolished in the 1890s. Granny Robertson's inn was a two-storied white washed house at the end of a row of cottages near the old bridge, on the present site of nos 9 and 11 Snuffmill Road. From the 1870s until 1894 travellers from the city could reach the inn by horse-drawn omnibus. Donnelly the coachman was a versifier for whom Cathcart was 'the most romantic village in the land' and he expressed his grief that 'the landmarks o' the village were wearin' fast away' in the following chorus:

> The auld hoose, the auld hoose,
> Close to the auld brig end,
> O mony a happy nicht's been spent,
> At the auld hoose in the glen.

The licence from Granny Robertson's was transferred to a public house 'The Auld Hoose', sited in a shop in the tenement at the corner of Old Castle Road and Crompton Avenue, until Cathcart became 'dry' in 1921, and thirsty locals had to take a tramcar to the Queen's Park Cafe in Victoria Road. The shop then became Kirkwood's bakery and the corner a splendid children's play area with a high wall for jinkers, a broad pavement for peevers and skipping ropes, a wide road for giant steps, gutters for bools and jorries, garden walls for high tig, and closes and back greens for hide and seek.

The 'green waving woods on the margin of Cart' inspired the landscape artist Alexander McBride to paint fine water-colours of woodland and riverside. The McBride family home was Cartbank, and Sandy McBride and his sister Elizabeth were the models for Sir John Lavery's picture *The Tennis Party* painted at Cartbank and exhibited in 1889. The painting is now in Aberdeen Art Gallery, and the Kelvingrove Gallery has a water-colour study *A Rally*, showing a lady player in mid-stroke, a novel pose for the time. Lavery also painted two historical pictures, *The Night after the Battle of Langside* and *The Morning after Langside*, which were sold abroad. Cartbank is an early 19th-century classical villa which looks over the Cart to the castle. For much of this century it was the home of the Macfarlane family, owners of the electrical engineering firm. The Linn Walkway passes along the riverside beneath Cartbank but the house, which is in private ownership, is not visible from below.

The Paper-makers

The pure and abundant water of the White Cart made paper-making an early and important industry at Cathcart. Paper-making was located at two mills: Millholm on the left bank of the river and Cathcart a little way downstream on the right bank beside the old bridge. These mills were known in the trade as numbers 18 and 19 respectively. The names of Deschamp, Hall and Couper are associated with no 18 and Lindsay with no 19. A third smaller paper mill upstream at Netherlee, operated by Archibald McGowan, became the Netherlee Printworks in the 1830s.

The forerunner of Millholm, and the first paper mill on the Cart, was established at Millbrae, near Langside, around 1686 by a Frenchman, Nicholas Deschamp, who had worked at mills at Dalry in Edinburgh and at Woodside in Glasgow. Ten years later Deschamp was sufficiently prosperous to contribute £100 sterling to the Darien scheme, and by 1729 had moved a mile upriver to larger premises at Millholm. Deschamp's daughter married James Hall, who afterwards carried on the business. In the peak years of Glasgow's tobacco trade the Halls converted from paper to snuff making at Millholm. According to the parish minister in 1793, this yielded a more certain and permanent profit. In 1835 it was reported that the paper mill was once again in full operation.

Millholm was sold in 1853 to Robert and James Couper, who had been tenants since 1841, employing around 30 men and boys and 60 women. The Coupers enlarged the premises and introduced machinery to produce high quality writing paper for banks, legal firms and HM Stationery Office. The mills were sold in 1884 as a going concern, and changed hands several times until finally closed in 1921 by Messrs Wiggins Teape & Co, bringing to an end over two hundred years of paper-making on the Cart. Part of the mill, including the 140 feet high chimney, was demolished in 1938. The remaining building continued in use as a flock mill until bought by the Macfarlane Engineering Company in 1947.

Robert and James Couper occupied Sunnyside and Holmwood, neighbouring houses on an elevated site above their mill, with fine views across the Cart to the castle and beyond. Robert married Mary Smith, daughter of the parish minister, and many Sunday School trips were held on the lawn at Sunnyside. Summers were spent at Dalmore, their home overlooking the Gareloch. Robert Couper died there in 1883 and is interred with his wife and son Archibald in Rhu kirkyard. Robert Couper left bequests worth £12,500 to his native village. This sum included the interest on £2,000 for the 'deserving poor' of Old and New Cathcart, and the interest on £1,000 for the 'better-class poor' of the parish of Cathcart. The legacy also provided for a hall, reading room and library for the people of Old and New Cathcart in the Couper Institute, a fine building designed by James Sellars and opened in 1887. The site on the west side of Clarkston Road was chosen as giving equal access to both communities. Alterations were made to the building in 1923 when the present Public Library was added.

In 1857 James Couper built Holmwood, choosing as his architect Alexander Thomson, who had just completed the Double Villa at Langside. Among the most interesting features introduced at Holmwood are the windows, constructed as a screen independently of the structural columns. This device is used to great effect in the dining-room to the right of the entrance and in the parlour to the left with its almost circular windows. The room above the parlour is the drawing room. At Holmwood Thomson used a long wall to link the house with the coachman's house to emphasise the strong horizontal lines of the main facade. Holmwood is now regarded by many as Thomson's finest villa.

A distinguished visitor to Holmwood in the 1920s was Lloyd George, who apparently bore a strong resemblance to the then owner, Bailie James Gray. In 1958 the house was sold to the Sisters of Our Lady of the Missions who built a school in the grounds. In

Holmwood was designed by Alexander Thomson for James Couper, owner of the Millholm Paper Mills. It is open on selected days while conservation is carried out by the National Trust for Scotland. To the left the parlour with drawing room above, and on the right the dining room.

1994 Holmwood was taken into the ownership of the National Trust for Scotland who are undertaking research and investigation which will be followed by conservation of the structure and the fine plaster work and stencilled and painted interior decoration. The house is open on selected days such as the annual Open Doors Day during the conservation programme

Cathcart Paper Mill, no 19, began in 1812 when Solomon Lindsay came from Penicuik and began the manufacture of paper in the former meal mill at the side of the old bridge. The chief manufacture was cardboard, at that time largely used for book-binding. The paper was made by hand and by machine. No 19 mill was a small enterprise, employing only 12 men in 1851, including Lindsay's two sons, James and David. In 1814 the manufacture of snuff was begun in a small portion of the buildings, the part with the gable to the end of the bridge, hence the popular name of the 'Old Snuff Mill'. This was a small scale activity carried on by James Hartley, who ground tobacco into snuff for city firms such as Messrs Stephen Mitchell, Smith and Hodge.

Lindsay House, the tall, narrow, three-storey, crow-stepped tenement on the north side of the bridge was designed in 1863 by John Baird II for David Lindsay, who was apparently thinking of marriage at the time. Lindsay intended to occupy the largest house which was entered by a side porch with a monogram above the door composed of all the letters of the name 'Lindsay'. This house occupied half of the ground floor and half of the basement. The other half of the basement contained the communal wash-house and coal cellars for the other five tenants . David never did wed and moved back across the road to live with his brother and sister Margaret in the little three roomed cottage beside the mill. Shortly after the death of David Lindsay in 1902 the mills closed and were sold to a Mr McIntosh who took down the cottage and built on the site the villa 'Mill House'. This was occupied by members of the McIntosh family until the 1970s. In 1976 the Cathcart Society saved the mill from demolition and ten years later the building was sold off to a developer.

Cathcart Parish Church and Manse

Cathcart Old Parish Church was opened in July 1929 and together with the remaining tower of its predecessor of 1831 in the old kirkyard across Carmunnock Road, it represents over a thousand years of continuous Christian worship on the site. A board inside the church informs us that the church was founded in the 9th century, attached to Paisley Abbey 1160–1560 and disjoined from the Presbytery of Paisley in 1596. The exact location of the medieval church is unknown, but beside it was St Oswald's well which was infilled when the graveyard was extended in the 19th century.

At the Reformation the Catholic priest, James Hill of Ibrox, conformed and remained at Cathcart until 1572, after which the church was under the charge of Protestant 'readers'. In 1586 Robert Hamilton, who had been reader for nine years, was raised to the status of minister and continued until his death in 1628. Later 17th-century ministers were increasingly embroiled in the religious and political controversies of the times. Gavin Forsyth left during the troubles in the time of Montrose; James Blair was charged with holding conventicles and killed in a shooting accident at Dalry in 1668; and on the eve of William of Orange's proclamation in Glasgow the parishioners revenged themselves on their 'obnoxious' minister, Robert Finnie, by kindling a bonfire at the manse and outing his wife and children. William Carstares, born in the manse of Cathcart in 1649, returned from exile with William and

*Only the belfry tower remains of the former Cathcart Parish Church built
in 1831. In the churchyard is the tomb of the Polmadie Martyrs.*

used his influence with the king in favour of Presbyterianism. He
is commemorated by a pillar in St Giles in Edinburgh where he
was minister, In Cathcart kirkyard the grave containing the remains
of the three martyrs shot at Polmadie in 1685 is another reminder
of the Killing Times.

   The first church known to us appears to have been erected in
1707 and rebuilt in 1744. A water-colour on display in Cathcart
Library shows this as a small rectangular building with a tall,
narrow tower attached to a crow-stepped front gable and a small
porch in front. This increasingly ruinous and inadequate church
was not replaced until a petition signed by 300 inhabitants of the

parish was delivered to the heritors in 1829 stating that the walls were beginning to bulge, and the roof to sink, the wood over the door on which the wall seems to rest being decayed and the crossbeam which supports the whole weight of the west gallery being bent and partly rotten. After much dragging of feet and complaints by Sir John Maxwell about the cost of a church 'in this unimportant parish, where the whole population does not extend to 2,000 souls' (as principal heritor Sir John had to pay out one third of the expenses), James Dempster was asked to draw up plans for a church for up to 750 sitters 'upon precisely the same design with the churches of Mauchline and Cardross' and the new church was finally opened in 1831. When the present church was built a century later there was again a dispute with the heritors and this was the last church in Scotland to be built under the old rule. The present church, dedicated to St Oswald, was designed by H E Clifford. The foundation stone was laid by John Buchan, Lord Tweedsmuir, a school friend of the minister, the Rev Dr John MacKellar.

Presumably the manse was repaired or replaced soon after the Finnie episode, for in 1793 the Rev David Dow wrote that the original structure was very old and had received many additions and repairs. In 1802 he sent the heritors a long list of necessary repairs costed at £350. The manse was continually damp and much decayed, the steps of the stair worn away in such a manner as to render it dangerous to ascend or descend, the office houses were ruinous and there was no barn, cellar, milk or cart house, the whole falling short of the accommodation which the family of a clergyman in these times required. A 'new and most commodious manse' was built, sixteen years later, with a three acre glebe and garden ground of one acre and a half stretching right down to the Cart with a considerable frontage along the river. Construction of the railway and new roads around 1900 spoiled the amenity of the manse and the Rev Arthur Caxton moved into the present manse in Carmunnock Road in 1905.

Palaces for dominies

The earliest known schoolmaster in Cathcart is Thomas Pettigrew who was appointed in accordance with an Act of 1696 restoring responsibility for schools to Presbyteries. On 16 June 1701 Pettigrew accepted the office of schoolmaster, precentor and

The Parish School stood at the top of Manse Brae until the 1930s. The oldest part dates from 1718; the larger schoolroom was added in 1798.

session clerk in return for an annual payment of one hundred merks: four pounds (equivalent of 60 merks) from the heritors, and 20 merks each from the session and the tenantry. In 1718 the session agreed to provide a schoolhouse, 'to be built instantly in the east end of the minister's yard where the old manse had stood'. This was a low stone house 18 feet long and 14 feet wide, with a small chamber at one end 'to serve as a retiring room for the heritors between sermons'.

There then followed from 1724 to 1746 a succession of dominies whose names are known to us, but who are otherwise shadowy figures: John Galloway who agreed to teach without fee 'such poor scholars whose parents are either dead or not able to pay their wages' (fees); William Gilmour who demitted in 1732, 'resolved to follow his books'; Patrick McCans; John Baird 'a student at the college of Glasgow'; Hugh Moodie; Patrick McAuslande; John Reid who left in 1744 to take up a post at Musselburgh Grammar; and James Porter. James Forsyth who came from Baldernock in 1746 had to produce testimonials. These were apparently satisfactory, for he was made an elder and remained as schoolmaster for 40 years. Next came Alexander Loudon and in 1790 James McClean who proved unsatisfactory and was replaced by William Dempster from 1792 until his death in 1822.

In Dempster's time there were 60 to 80 scholars who were taught reading, English grammar, writing, arithmetic and book keeping, but 'it was seldom that a classical education is required, and parents, whose circumstances enable them to procure it for their children, repair to Glasgow'. In 1798 the session agreed to raise Dempster's salary from 120 to 200 merks (about £10 sterling), the maximum appointed by law. They also agreed to build a new schoolhouse and give Dempster and his family the old building as a dwelling instead of the 12 foot square heritors' room where they appear to have been living. Unfortunately by 1829 the low, damp situation and the earthen floors, plus the fact that the ridge lead had been taken away from the new roofs, made both buildings uncomfortable and injurious to health. Eventually a complete new school and schoolmaster's house were erected on a new site in 1830. These were demolished in the 1890s to make way for the tenements facing the kirkyard at the top of Kilmailing Road. The original school buildings of 1718 and 1798 remained at the top of Manse Brae until demolished around 1938.

Dempster's successor was James Bell and the last parochial schoolmaster of Cathcart was the much respected Andrew Carnduff, a native of Tarbolton, who held the post from 1846 until a new school and schoolhouse were built in 1876 at Craig Road by the newly formed Cathcart Parish School Board. Mr Carnduff continued as Session Clerk and Registrar until his death in 1894 aged 77 years.

An industrial giant: G & J Weir & Co

Until 1886 the main employers in Cathcart were the paper mills and Geddes's Dyeworks and Carpet factory. Geddes's Works were located on the left bank of the Cart just below Cathcart New Bridge and the tall works chimney was a local landmark. Around 1850 the works employed about 100 men and another 50 women, boys and girls. By the 1880s the business was in decline and the works were demolished and a square of tenements, Holmhead Crescent, Street, Terrace and Place, built on the site. William Geddes resided at Holmhead House and later at Battlefield House. His brother and partner John Geddes built Thornbank, a house which has now

A group of workers at Weirs Works during the First World War when women helped to manufacture shells and aircraft.

been demolished and replaced by an apartment block at the corner of Clarkston Road and Monteith Road East.

A few other small firms were concentrated in the vicinity of the dyeworks. These included the intriguingly named Cassels Gold Extracting Company managed by H A Jones. Verel's photographic works were managed by Francis William Verel of the Verel family who occupied Linn House. The head of this talented and enterprising family was a naturalised Frenchman, William Aristides Verel, manager of the large Tharsis Sulphur and Copper Company located at St Rollox. Linn House is currently used by Glasgow Parks Department as a nature centre for the Linn Park.

Cathcart's little international business community also included the Dutchman Heinziens Koopmans, churn master at the Cathcart Creamery, manufacturers of margarine. The six Koopmans children were Wilhelmina, Antonius, Petronella, Theodorus, Hendrikens and little Maria.

A new era began for Cathcart in 1886 with the arrival of what was to become, and still is, Cathcart's major employer, then the engineering partnership of G & J Weir, today Weir Pumps, part of the large international Weir Group. The firm was begun by George and James Weir at Liverpool in 1871 and transferred two years later to Hydepark Street in Anderston. At first G & J Weir & Co were consulting engineers with no productive capacity of their own. In 1866, however, the brothers set up the Holm Foundry at Cathcart with a machine shop, brass foundry and a smithy, employing 14 men to manufacture their own products. Weir's business was founded principally on a group of inventions designed to increase the efficiency of marine boilers, with the firm supplying auxiliary machinery and pumps to home and foreign shipbuilders including the Admiralty.

In 1898 the works were enlarged on a five acre site and the following year William Weir, the eldest son of James Weir, became managing director at the age of 22 years. William bought his first car, a $3^{1}/_{2}$hp Benz around this time and then ventured into car production. Weirs built three racing cars for Darracq at Cathcart which competed without success in the Isle of Man races in 1904 but a possible deal with the Hon C S Rolls fell through when Rolls chose Henry Royce as his partner instead. James Weir handed over control of the company to his sons William and George in 1910 and two years later new offices were built on Newlands Road in an imposing building which was a copy of the factory of the Packard Automobile Company of Detroit. The Minto building was built round the corner in Inverlair Avenue the following year to a design by the same American architect, Moritz Kahn. The east office block in Newlands Road was added around 1950 and includes the clock-tower at the entrance to a 1930s design.

At the outbreak of war in 1914 the Albert and Flanders factories were erected at Cathcart employing 3,000 workers to manufacture shells. Production later switched to the National Projectile Factory at Cardonald. Weirs then used the Albert Factory to build aircraft, complete with engines, to other companies' designs and with over a thousand aircraft completed by mass production techniques, Weirs became the largest Clydeside producer of military aircraft during the war. In 1915 William Weir resigned as managing director to take up a government post with the Ministry of Munitions and subsequently became Secretary of State for the RAF. He was awarded a peerage in 1918. The company, with William Weir back at the helm, continued its interest in aircraft during the interwar period by developing an autogiro and in 1938 producing the Weir helicopter. The firm also attempted to diversify their products by constructing pre-fabricated steel housing in their factory at

Cardonald in the 1920s and again at Coatbridge in the late 1940s.

Prior to the Second World War William Weir advised successive Governments about matters of industry and was created Viscount Weir of Eastwood in 1938. During the war Weirs again played a major role, employing 4,000 men and 1,200 women in their four establishments at Cathcart, Yoker, Thornliebank and Slough. Cathcart received a royal visit in February 1940 when the King and Queen inspected one of the famous 25 pounder field gun carriages under production. Mrs Eleanor Roosevelt visited Cathcart in November 1942 and is said to have been particularly impressed by the number of women in the works. The factory at Yoker was extensively damaged by enemy bombing in 1941 but Cathcart was unscathed, although surviving German maps show it to have been a prime target.

After the war the management was reorganised in favour of the third generation, with W Kenneth Weir becoming managing director in 1946, then chairman on the retiral of his father in 1954. Holm Foundry was closed and the space used for the manufacture of new sea-water and distillation plant. The Weir Group is today a holding company for a group involved in two main areas of business, engineering products and engineering services and is one of Britain's top companies. Weir Pumps Ltd is a subsidiary with over 2,000 employees, manufacturing centrifugal pumps, electric motors and ancillary equipment for markets in the Near and Ear East and in Asia, at their works in Cathcart and branches in Scotland and England.

The other major employer in Cathcart was the Wallace-Scott Tailoring Institute built as a garden factory and completed in 1922 to a design by Sir J J Burnet. The Institute was notable for the facilities provided for employees with rest lounges, a dining hall, and baths and washbasins with hot and cold water. Sadly, the gardens, tennis courts, bowling greens and sports ground disappeared when the site was extensively redeveloped by the South of Scotland Electricity Board as their headquarters in the 1950s. It is now the headquarters of Scottish Power.

The Cathcart Circle: after the Polis Force the greatest thing in Glesca

The year 1886 is a double landmark in the history of Cathcart, for in the same year as Weirs built the Holm Foundry, the Cathcart District Railway was extended from Mount Florida to Cathcart. The original station was on the right bank of the river, with access from the top of Manse Brae. When the line was extended westwards to complete the Cathcart Circle in 1894, the station was removed across the river to its present site and the old station became the goods yard. Access to the new passenger station was by two subways at either end of the platform. The entrance from Old Castle Road by an iron foot bridge over the river is now closed. In 1903 the Lanarkshire and Ayrshire Railway (the L & A) built a second line immediately to the south of Cathcart station to carry coal from Newton to Ardrossan for shipping. The L & A was then linked up to the Circle just west of Cathcart station to provide a passenger route from Glasgow Central to the coast. The 9.05 from Central called at Cathcart to pick up at 9.18, and arrived at Ardrossan at 9.57 for the Arran steamer. This line now terminates at Neilston.

Rail travel proved immediately popular and by the turn of the century there was a train every 10 minutes on the Circle. The Cathcart Omnibus was withdrawn in 1894, having plied between Cathcart and the city for more than 20 years. However there was stiff competition from the tramways, particularly after Battlefield Electric Tram Depot opened at the foot of Holmlea Road in 1901. The railway reduced their fares but it was not until the Bridge Street terminus was replaced in 1905 by the new spacious Glasgow Central station that rail traffic recovered.

The first station-master at Cathcart was Mr John Cowper and the first ticket to Glasgow was purchased on the morning of 25 May 1886 by the local postmaster, John McGaw. John Cowper was succeeded in 1888 by Mr W J Munro, a popular figure who remained at Cathcart for 28 years. A great feature of the Circle stations were F W Wilson's bookstalls. Cathcart's was the first, but the stall disappeared when it was blown off the platform during a gale on a December night in 1894. Much confusion arose in the early days between the Outer and Inner Circles, especially as the stations all looked alike and were dimly lit. Another hazard were the city schoolboys who 'shouted, screamed, whistled, groaned, shoved and smashed' not in one compartment, but all over the train wherever an empty compartment was to be found. The Cathcart Circle even inspired a novel, *Snooker Tam of the Cathcart Railway*, written by R W Campbell in 1919. It tells the tale of Tam the boy porter, Maggie McCheery the ticket girl, and Maister McMuckle the station-master at a fictional station called Kirkbride, and their adventures with Italian spies. Mr McMuckle had a nod for every under-dog, and his bonnet off to every lady with the latest Treron fashions. It was untrue that the railway was specially built 'for high heid yins in insurance offices, public-hooses, and drapers' shops'. On the contrary. The Circle was the Circle of Romance, 'a deadly trap for bachelors and the hope of the pretty typists', where on the 'five-thirty' could be seen 'everything from a Geisha to a Madonna'. After the 'Polis Force' claimed Tam, the Cathcart Railway is the greatest thing in 'Glesca'. Unfortunately real tragedy struck in December 1945 when three railway staff were shot in the station-master's room at Pollokshields East station. The clerkess and boy porter died, while an older porter-clerk escaped injury. The assailant, a railway fireman, suffering from schizophrenia, later gave himself up.

Road communications were also developed at the end of last century. The Hunchback Bridge was removed in 1900 and the keystone found to bear an inscription 'Built by James Allison, 1799–1800'. It was replaced by the present red granite Cathcart New Bridge. The work was carried out to facilitate the extension of the tramway to Netherlee. A few years later Delvin Road was laid out and a new bridge built over the Cart to form a new east-west route from Carmunnock Road to Clarkston Road. The realignment of Manse Brae and the construction of the Delvin Road Bridge destroyed part of the manse garden which until then had extended right down to the river.

Survivors of the past

New industry and the new rail and road links with the city led to the building of suburban villas, terraced houses and tenements. This laid the foundations of a well balanced 20th-century social structure in Cathcart, complemented by public buildings, churches and schools, several of which survive to the present day. Unlike many areas where Church of Scotland buildings have been converted to other use or demolished, and congregations amalgamated, Cathcart Old Parish Church, Cathcart South and Cathcart New have so far survived the 20th century intact. The oldest building in use is Cathcart South, completed in 1894 on a site close to the Couper Institute by a United Presbyterian congregation formed in 1887. This congregation took an early interest in youth work and within seven years had formed a Band of Hope, the 1st Cathcart (85th Glasgow) Company of the Boys' Brigade, and had opened its doors to an already existing branch of the Foundry Boys. A Missionary Society was begun in 1889 and among the distinguished visitors were Mary Slessor from Calabar and Eric Liddell, hero of 'Chariots of Fire' who spoke of his mission work in China in 1940. The congregation of Cathcart New in Newlands Road was formed in 1899 in connection with the Free Church Extension Movement, and a year later became a United Free Church. An earlier Free Church congregation became Battlefield East.

The members of the United Free Church who remained outside the union with the Church of Scotland in 1929 today worship in their church in Struan Road under the Rev J D Neil. The congregation of Cathcart Baptist Church was formed in 1923 and opened a hall-church two years later in Merrylee Road, to which an extension was added in 1954. The organ was installed as a War Memorial in 1948. Cathcart Congregational Church in Holmlea Road was opened in 1935. Christ the King RC Church was completed in 1960 in Carmunnock Road and is a modern brick building with a striking relief of Christ the King on the front facing the King's Park. Other places of Christian worship are Kingdom Hall on the former site of the Rialto cinema in Old Castle Road and the Brethern's Meeting Room at Braehead. There is also a synagogue in Merrylee Road and the Jewish Cemetery in Netherlee Road was opened in 1925.

Nothing now remains of Craig Road school, the first school to be built by the Cathcart School Board in 1876 with John Imrie FEIS as headmaster, and which later became St Oswald's Special School. The oldest remaining school building is the handsome Holmlea Primary, erected in 1908. Still alive in Cathcart folk-memory are the names of infant mistress Miss McColl, Daddy Robertson, Daddy Muir, Miss McLean and the 'old' and the 'young' Misses McGillivray. More recent primary schools are Simshill, Merrylee in Ashmore

Morning break at Holmlea Primary School. This fine red-sandstone school was built in 1908.

Road, St Mirin's in Carmunnock Road and St Fillan's in Crompton Avenue. Two secondary schools were built in the 1960s: King's Park, transferred from its original hilltop site in King's Park Avenue to modern buildings on an even steeper site in Carmunnock Road; and St Oswald's, built on similarly sloping ground on the site of the old Craig Road school.

No community worth its salt in the 1930s was without its cinema and Cathcart had three, the Rialto, the Kingsway and the Toledo. The Toledo in Clarkston Road is the sole survivor. Cathcart cinema-goers favoured all things Spanish, and the Toledo was given balcony effects on the frontage and Spanish decor inside as well as a Spanish name. In 1974 over 8,000 local people signed a petition to stop the cinema becoming a Bingo Hall. The Toledo is now a three-screen cinema renamed the Cannon. The Kingsway in Cathcart Road was built in 1929 with a Hispanic-style foyer curved along the street. It was one of George Singleton's chain of Vogue cinemas, became the Vogue Bingo and now stands empty. The Rialto began as the Cathcart Picture House in the days of the silent films. No Spanish architecture, but its very own orchestra — Willie Wilson's six-piece band. It finished life as the George cinema and is now demolished. Other recreational facilities include the

Cathcart Bowling Club which celebrated its centenary in 1989. The Old Men's Club in Old Castle Road was gifted in 1935 by ex-councillor Frederick Shoesmith who lived in nearby Hawthorn Lodge, and named Edith Cottage after his wife. The Swing Park at Holmlea Road still provides a safe children's play area.

Within Old Cathcart village the 'smithy or cartwright establishment' admired by MacDonald and his ramblers has survived many changes of use. The village smiths were the Peddies, hereditary armourers to the Earls of Cathcart. Robert Peddie, last of the family, was a veterinary surgeon and used the upper flat of the smiddy as a Dog Infirmary. This was reached by an outside stair, now removed. The smiddy is now a licensed restaurant, and MacDonald would undoubtedly approve of this 'exceedingly neat and comfortable little place of rest and refreshment'. Adjacent to the smiddy, the 'handsome farm-steading' of MacDonald's time survived until the 1950s. This was the dwelling house of the 80 acre Castle Mains farm which was occupied last century by families of Russells and Youngs and then by Robert Peddie and finally by Robert Ure until his death in 1958.

Only a few traces survive of the once extensive paper manufactory that was Millholm, but the buildings of the snuff mill at the bridge have worn well and are presently being converted into housing. Lindsay House remains intact. Ramblers can still enjoy the charms of rural beauty and quietude in the Linn Park and along the riverside walk from the old bridge upriver to Netherlee. And those two ancient landmarks — the kirkyard and the river crossing — still mount guard at either end of the village that is Cathcart.

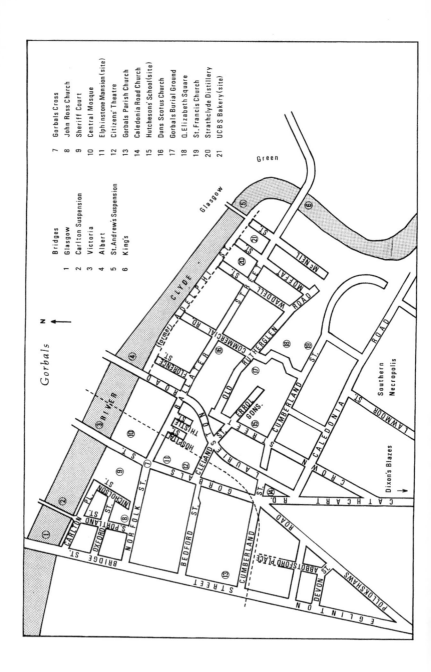

Gorbals

N

Bridges
1 Glasgow
2 Carlton Suspension
3 Victoria
4 Albert
5 St.Andrew's Suspension
6 King's

7 Gorbals Cross
8 John Ross Church
9 Sheriff Court
10 Central Mosque
11 Elphinstone Mansion (site)
12 Citizens' Theatre
13 Gorbals Parish Church
14 Caledonia Road Church
15 Hutchesons' School (site)
16 Duns Scotus Church
17 Gorbals Burial Ground
18 Q.Elizabeth Square
19 St.Francis Church
20 Strathclyde Distillery
21 UCBS Bakery (site)

CHAPTER 3
GORBALS

Gorbals began as a village in the parish of Govan from which it was disjoined in 1771, and in pre-Reformation times came under the authority of the Bishops of Glasgow. It was originally known as Little Govan to distinguish it from Meikle Govan, the Govan of today. The village was also known as Bridgend, taking this name from a stone bridge of eight arches which Bishop Rae built over the Clyde in 1345. It also served as an isolation colony for lepers for whom Lady Lochow is traditionally believed to have founded a hospital shortly after the bridge was built. Two derivations for the name Gorbals have been put forward: from the Latin word *garbale* meaning teinds paid to the church in the form of sheaves of grain; or from the Gaelic words *garbh ball* meaning a rough plot of ground.

The hospital was dedicated to St Ninian and was supported by the church and by gifts. King James IV, during a visit to Glasgow in 1491, gave 20 shillings in alms 'to the sick folk at the brig of Glasgow'. In 1589 'the Lepers' House at the Gorbals end of the bridge' contained six lepers; Andrew Lawson, merchant; Steven Gilmour, cordiner; Robert Bogle, son of Patrick Bogle; Patrick Brittal, tailor; John Thomson, tailor; Daniel Cunningham, tinker. The hospital was still in use in 1610 when an entry in the Glasgow Burgh records states:

> It is statut and ordainit that the lipper of the Hospital sall gang only upon the calsie syde, near the gutter, and sal haif clapperis, and ane claith upon their mouth and face, and sall stand afar of qul (while) they resaif almons or answer, under the payne of banisching tham the toun and Hospitall.

After the Reformation the church feued the village and lands of Gorbals to Sir George Elphinstone, merchant and provost of Glasgow, who had them erected into a Burgh of Barony and Regality. Sir George found Gorbals sufficiently attractive to enclose part of St Ninian's Croft for an orchard and garden and erect a house and chapel at the north-east corner of Gorbals Main Street and Rutherglen Loan. Elphinstone 'lived in great state and died in great poverty'. The barony was sold to Lord Belhaven who added a square three storey tower with turrets at each corner to the north side of Sir George's property. In 1650 the lands of Gorbals were purchased by the Town Council of Glasgow in partnership with the Trades House and Hutchesons' Hospital, and the baronial buildings became 'the tounes houss and tour in Gorballs'. This was the head-quarters of the Glasgow bailie who ruled Gorbals until the burgh was formally annexed in 1846. These were handsome buildings, and served the community as court-house, police office, prison, assembly hall and school before degenerating into squalid dwellings and a public house which were finally swept away by the City Improvement Trust in 1866.

After 1790 Tradeston and Hutchesontown were developed for industry and Laurieston was planned as a residential suburb. These districts, as well as the old Gorbals village in the centre, were soon blighted as residential areas by the intrusion of industrial premises and railways, and by overcrowding as waves of destitute immigrants flocked into the area in search of work. Those who prospered moved out to suburbs further south. In 1957 Gorbals was designated a Comprehensive Development Area with the destruction of most older buildings and the dispersal of most of its population. Regeneration is now under way and a new 'Gorbals Village' is being created which will surely achieve its aim of attracting back people who will be proud to live once again at the heart of this historic community.

The eighteenth-century village: on the brink of change

In his account of Gorbals parish in 1793, the Rev William Anderson describes how the village had grown since the beginning of the 18th century. At that time Gorbals consisted only of a few thatched houses along Main Street, mainly occupied by maltmen who made malt and brewed ale. By 1730 new houses for weavers had filled up the spaces, but the village had been destroyed by fire in 1748. Good houses were then built, some of two storeys and others of three storeys and garrets, and by 1771 the village contained 3,000 persons. Now in 1793, besides many weavers, Gorbals also contained gunsmiths, nailers, shoemakers, tailors, wrights and cotton spinners. Examples of flintlock fowling pieces and pocket pistols made by one family of Gorbals gunsmiths, the Manns, can be seen in the Kelvingrove Art Gallery and Museum. John

McArthur's *Plan of the City of Glasgow, Gorbells & Caltoun* shows the village of Gorbals in 1778.

According to John Ord, the historian of Gorbals, the inhabitants bought a piece of land on the south side of Rutherglen Loan in 1715 to be used as a burial ground, but it was not until 1729 that a Chapel of Ease was erected in the village in Buchan Street. This served for worship until a new church was built in Carlton Place in 1810, after which the Chapel was used by a Gaelic congregation. William Anderson became the first minister of the parish of Gorbals when it was disjoined from Govan in 1771, but the burial ground remained for many years a detached portion of Gorbals parish. Several of the old tombstones round the walls have trade symbols: one with crossed shovels, denoting a baker, and another a miller, are both dated 1723. Later stones commemorate John Mackenzie, minister of the Gaelic Chapel, and the schoolmaster John Wilson, reputedly the Dr Hornbook of Burns's poem *Death and Dr Hornbook*. Also buried here is Walter Neilson, Engineer, of Govan Colliery, father of James Beaumont Neilson of Hot Blast fame, and grandfather of 'Wee Walter' Neilson, who founded the Hyde Park Locomotive Works.

In the 18th century the responsibility for maintaining law and order in the barony lay with a Gorbals depute bailie appointed from among their number by the Glasgow magistrates. The bailies, described as 'veritable terrors to wrong-doers' were empowered to fine, imprison and whip law breakers, and as a last resort banish 'incorrigibles' from the barony. The Black Book of the Gorbals records banishments from 1749 till 1791. Punishment was made legal by the offender signing the page, or more usually making his or her mark. In the earlier cases banishment was usually for life. In the 1750s Janet Leyle and Ann McGibon 'found seling and disposing of a large bras Candlestik' are banished 'for all time cuming', as are also Mary Fleming for stealing a pair of sheets and a woman's skirt, Mary Campble 'found in Luse company' and Catrine Matthie for 'keeping a bade houss and Eivell Company'. The ritual of banishment was carried out on James McArthur, a Gorbals blacksmith and Jean Stevenson, his wife in 1775 when at precisely 12 o'clock on 16 September the pair were taken from the common prison in the chapel of Gorbals, and by tuck of drum and with heads bare and uncovered, were banished from the village and barony of Gorbals during the whole of their natural

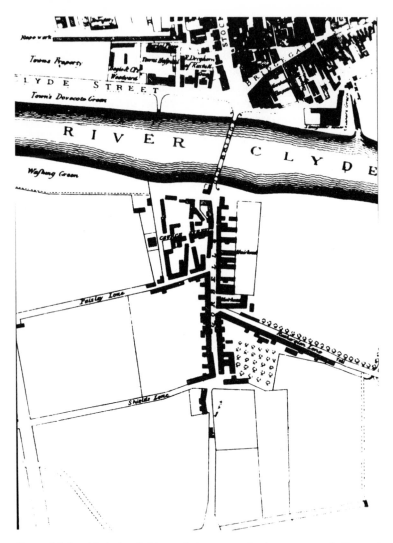

Part of John McArthur's Plan of the City of Glasgow, Gorbells and Caltoun, *showing the village of Gorbals in 1778.*

lives. The pair had admitted the charge of 'keeping a disreputable house, of receiving and entertaining in it people of bad character, and of cursing, swearing, making noise, alarming and disturbing their neighbours at unseasonable hours etc'. Later cases were dealt with more leniently. For stealing or taking away a shirt from

Pollokshaws in 1764, Hellean Brookes was banished for seven years. In one of the last recorded cases, William Gilmour, weaver, 'for stealing a hen and a duck and giving them to Janet Stewart to sell which she accordingly did' got off with a warning, perhaps because 'the hen and Duck was got again and no harm done to them'.

In 1793 the minister recorded that there were 60 public houses in the village 'which hurt the morals of the people not a little'. There is no mention of the new distillery in Kirk Street, said to have been founded in 1786 by William Menzies, the first distiller granted a licence in the west of Scotland after the passing of an act requiring distilleries to be operated only by respectable tenants. In concluding his report, Mr Anderson foresees the great changes about to take place in his parish-:

> The barony of Gorbals is begun to be feued. There are plans for new streets on the east and west of the old village, which, at a moderate computation, will contain upwards of 50,000 inhabitants. The feuing goes on briskly; there are upwards of 120 steadings already feued, and begun to build on.

In fact the actual population of Gorbals reached 40,000 by 1891 and by the 1930s had risen to 90,000.

Gorbals village in the nineteenth century

In the optimistic atmosphere of the early 19th century, the impending increase of population was viewed as an advantage to Gorbals. It gave an opportunity to establish a new residential suburb to the west which would become Laurieston, and an industrial area to the east which would bring employment and prosperity to the new district of Hutchesontown. Wedged in the centre, the old village of Gorbals bore the brunt of the sharp rise in population and faced the task of dealing with the resultant social problems as best it could. The care of the poor was made impossible by the number of beggars and vagrants claiming to live in the Gorbals. According to a broad-sheet sold by Hawkie, the well-known street-character from Calton across the Clyde, those who had three-pence to pay for a bed had an open door at Molly Gillespie's, an Irish woman who kept a lodging house of 13 beds which were full every night, besides two beds she kept for those who could not pay. Over a period of 30 years, 50,000 lodgers had spent the night under Molly's hospitable roof, tinkers, beggars,

Gorbals Main Street looking south, from William Simpson's Glasgow in
the Forties. *The square tower was part of Sir George Elphinstone's Baronial
Mansion at the corner of Rutherglen Loan. This building later served as
the town-house of Gorbals.*

fortune-tellers, 'Rowly powley Gentry' and a host of other travelling
characters. Laurieston and Hutchesontown were outwith Gorbals
parish and their poor and insane were the responsibility of Govan
parish, and housed in the Govan poor-house, a former Cavalry
Barracks on the west side of Eglinton Street. Gorbals and Govan
parishes were combined for poor Law purposes when a new
poorhouse was opened at Merryflats in 1872.

Some idea of the stress caused by the enormity of the task is
conveyed by the epitaph on the tombstone of the Rev James
McLean DD, who succeeded Mr Anderson. Dr McLean died in 1833
and is buried in the Gorbals burial-ground:

> His ministerial labours in Gorbals commenced in the year 1793 when
> the population of the parish was 5,000; at the period of his decease it
> reached 35,000; during nearly thirty years the management of the poor
> of the parish was left entirely in the hands of himself and of the Kirk
> Session...probably he united in marriage more couples and adminis-
> trated the sacrament of baptism to more children, than any other
> clergyman of the Established Church of Scotland.

In 1808 Gorbals was given permission to operate its own police
force and the burgh took over the old mansion house of the

Gorbals Parish Church from William Simpson's Glasgow in the Forties. The church was built in 1810 and for over a century its 174-foot-high spire was a landmark on the riverside at the east end of Carlton Terrace.

Elphinstones as a police office. After 1826 law and order was effected from a new Baronial Building at the corner of South Portland and Norfolk Streets. When Gorbals, Anderston and Calton were annexed to the city in 1846, their police forces were amalgamated with the Glasgow force, and Gorbals became the South Division. A new police office and barracks were built in Oxford Street at Nicholson Street in 1895 to a design of A B Macdonald, the City Engineer. This building is now used as the Strathclyde Police Training Centre. The Gorbals force is now part of Strathclyde's F Division and is accommodated in a modern building in

Cumberland Street.

After the annexation to Glasgow the problem of overcrowding was tackled with vigour. In 1848 the Glasgow authorities were seized by a 'dinging-doun' fever after a city centre sugar-refining house collapsed with the loss of 14 lives. In Gorbals Main Street a building known as the 'Community Land' was demolished after the Dean of Guild Inspectors arrived to find an Irish wake still in progress after the front wall had given way in a cloud of dust during the night with the 20 mourners crammed into one small apartment and the corpse laid out in the corner. Part of the old Baronial Mansion was demolished in 1848 and the remainder swept away with the rest of Old Gorbals when the City Improvement Trust formed Gorbals Cross in the 1870s.

In one respect Gorbals was ahead of the rest of Glasgow. In 1848 the Gorbals Gravitation Water Company brought pure and wholesome water to Gorbals and other south side districts from the Brock Burn and other streams and lochs in Renfrewshire six miles away. This was a decade before Loch Katrine water was led into the north of the City.

Laurieston

In 1801 James Laurie, a merchant who had made good in London, feued land to the west of Gorbals village from the Hutchesons' Trustees and began to lay out the new suburb of Laurieston. Laurie hoped to attract as residents business and professional gentlemen who would have easy access to the city from Gorbals Main Street to the Bridgegate by the old bridge, or from Bridge Street to the Broomielaw by the new bridge which had been opened in 1772. The latter was replaced in 1833 by an even more splendid bridge designed by Thomas Telford, 60 feet in width and 'wider than any river bridge in the Kingdom'. While this work was under way a convenient wooden foot-bridge was built across the river at South Portland Street. All these bridges now have modern replacements. The foot-bridge was replaced by a handsome iron suspension bridge constructed in 1871 to a design by Alexander Kirkland.

Building began in Carlton Place, laid out as a prestigious street along the side of the river and named after the London residence of the Prince Regent. The first two terraces were designed by the London architect Peter Nicholson, after whom Nicholson Street is named. The east terrace was built in 1804–8; the west terrace followed in 1818. Laurieston House, in the centre of the east terrace, was built as a double mansion for Laurie and his brother and was considered the most elegant house in the city. Its special features are the exceptionally fine plasterwork and the staircase with a balcony from which ladies could before dances, it is said, keep an eye on arrivals in the entrance hall below. The building was restored in 1988 by the Strathclyde Building Preservation Trust and is presently unoccupied. Numbers 71–73 Carlton Place were internally remodelled as the Prince and Princess of Wales Hospice, the city's wedding gift to the royal couple. During restoration the original cast-iron railings and lamp standards in the street were refurbished and stone setts reinstated.

The principal street leading south from Carlton Place was South Portland Street and its southern extension, Abbotsford Place. Most of this broad street was swept away after 1970. The tenements erected in Abbotsford Place were spacious and much favoured as residences by doctors. These buildings were of unique design with Italianate Renaissance frontages and traditional Scottish circular stair-towers of brick at the back. This wide and elegant street was blighted by an overhead railway bridge built for the City of Glasgow Union Railway in the 1860s which intersected Abbotsford Place just south of Cumberland Street. The intrusion of railway tracks and terminals and industry hastened the middle class exodus from Laurieston and led to the subdivision and over-crowding of the once fashionable houses. Abbotsford School, which is still in use as the local primary school at the corner of Abbotsford Place and Devon Street, is an example of the former elegance and dignity of the district. It was built in 1879 to a design by H & D Barclay, with all the ground floor rooms opening off a central hall and the upper rooms entered from a balcony, and became a blue-print for many Glasgow schools.

Work began in 1806 on David Hamilton's imposing Parish Church at the east end of Carlton Place and in 1810 the congregation moved from the Chapel of Ease in Buchan Street. For more than a century and a half the soaring 174 feet high spire formed a landmark on the river bank, although it was not rebuilt to its full height after suffering severe damage by lightning in 1929. At the Disruption the greater part of the congregation 'came out' and formed John Knox Free Church. The father of the author, John Buchan, was minister of John Knox from 1888 to 1911. Gorbals

Parish and John Knox were reunited in 1943. A long line of ministers led worship in this building until demolition in 1973. The new Sheriff Court now occupies the site. The Rev William McPherson and his congregation then moved to the present parish church in Eglinton Street where they formed a new Gorbals congregation with members of Laurieston-Renwick, Abbotsford-Chalmers and St Ninian's-Wynd churches. All these older churches are now demolished. A little to the south of the new parish church, Eglinton Congregational Church in Eglinton Street and the former Chalmers Free Church in Pollokshaws Road have survived, but both are now closed as churches. The James Shields Project has converted Chalmers into 40 flats for young people. The former Gorbals Library in Norfolk Street is now used for worship by the congregation of the John Ross Memorial Church for the Deaf. The building houses the offices of the Glasgow and West of Scotland Society for the Deaf, who use it as a day centre and sports centre.

Hutchesontown (1); industry

The development of Hutchesontown, to the east of Gorbals village, began in 1790. Streets were laid out on a grid plan and pride of place along the riverside was given to Adelphi Street and Adelphi Place, named in honour of George and Thomas Hutcheson, founders of Hutchesons' Hospital, from the Greek word 'adelphi' meaning 'brothers'. Hospital Street was formed at right angles to Adelphi Street, but after the Hutchesontown Bridge was built across to the Saltmarket in 1794, Crown Street became the principal north-south thoroughfare. The river is now crossed at this point by the Albert Bridge built in 1872. The new main route south through Hutchesontown incorporates part of Hospital Street and part of Crown Street and is confusingly named Laurieston Road.

The spinning and weaving of cotton quickly became the most important of the new industries in Hutchesontown. Eleven mills were in operation around 1860, four engaged in powerloom weaving only and seven in both spinning and weaving. The two largest were Neale Thomson's Adelphi Works between Adelphi Street and Rose (now Florence) Street, and William Higginbotham's Wellington Mill between Govan (now Ballater) Street and Commercial Road. These two sites are now occupied by the former Adelphi Public School and the former St Luke's Church (now Blessed John Duns Scotus). Many of the mill workers came across the river from Calton and Bridgeton, at first by ferry and after 1855 by the St Andrew's suspension bridge. The bridge also served the workers in the dyeworks and print fields situated in the bend of the river opposite Glasgow Green. The Ordnance Survey map of 1859 shows, along this stretch of the river from east to west, the Springfield Print Works, Adelphi Dye Works, Clydesvale Silk and Woollen Mills, Govanhaugh Dye Works and the Albyn Cotton Works. This was the area which in the 1860s was still known as 'Little Govan'. It was described at the time as a suburban village and precisely defined as consisting of York (Moffat) Street, Upper Govan (east part of Ballater) Street, Hayfield Street and McNeil Street.

Just to the west of Moffat Street was Stonefield House and its garden and ornamental grounds. This was the property of Mr Thom, who owned a large weaving factory on the east side of Commercial Road. The 'substantial old mansion-house of Stonefield' later became a hotel and the grounds were used until the turn of the century as a games field for bowling, cricket and foot-races. The little green oasis was eventually developed for shops and houses in Lawmoor, Mathieson and Waddell Streets, the last named after the developer, James Waddell. The area is now covered by the multi-storey flats built in 1965 at Waddell Court and Commercial Court.

In 1860 a second 'industrial zone' existed between Florence Street and Commercial Road, as far south as Old Rutherglen Road. In addition to the cotton mills and weaving factories, this area contained the Clyde Flour Mill, a starch and gum works, a hair and fur factory, a bleaching works, a chemical works, a saw mill, a biscuit factory 'in which bickets are baked by machinery', the Clutha Iron Works, a large foundry operated by Gourlay & Co, a smithy and a small brewery owned by Mr Rutherford on the west side of Commercial Road. The sole survivor of all this industry is one cotton mill built in 1816 at the corner of Commercial Road and Old Rutherglen Road and owned in 1860 by a Mr Logan. This was latterly a factory producing Twomax knitwear, a brand name adapted from the surnames of the two partners, McClure and McIntosh. The building is presently being renovated to become a modern business centre. In the 1860s there were only open fields between Rutherglen Road and Dixon's Blazes except for a rope works, the Gorbals burial ground, the Southern Necropolis and

Part of Strathclyde Distillery being demolished before rebuilding in the late 1970s. The tenements in Ballater Street were built for their workers by the Co-operative Society and are still occupied. The St Mungo's Halls behind have been demolished.

Hutchesontown Gardens, an area of small allotments used for growing fruit and vegetables.

The part of Hutchesontown from Florence Street west to Gorbals Main Street was occupied in the 1860s by housing with almost no industry except for the Adelphi Distillery on a two acre site close to the river banks. This was the old St Ninian's Croft, the probable site of the leper hospital, and had been a fine orchard until the trees were cut down in 1826 and the distillery begun by C & D Gray. When Alfred Barnard described his tour of inspection in his *Whisky Distillers of the United Kingdom*, the proprietors were A Walker & Co and the annual output for the season 1884–5 was over 500,000 gallons. Barnard was shown the two still houses, one containing a Coffey patent still for the production of grain whisky and the other a fine, lofty and well-lighted building containing four handsome pot stills for the production of malt. The name of the distillery was later changed to 'Loch Katrine' as the proprietors considered that the Loch Katrine water they used 'contained all the properties necessary for the making of good whisky'. The distillery was taken over by the Distillers Company in 1902 and closed, but the warehouses were retained until the 1960s. The site is now occupied by the Glasgow Central Mosque. Strathclyde Distillery on the riverside between Waddell Street and Moffat Street was established as a grain distillery by a subsidiary of Seager, Evans & Co in 1927. From 1957–75 this distillery also produced Kinclaith Malt Whisky, taking the name from the former croft on the opposite side of the Clyde. Strathclyde was extensively rebuilt after 1975 and is now owned by Allied Distillers who produce spirit for blending in several whiskies including Long John.

Another great enterprise in Hutchesontown was the United Co-operative Bakery in McNeil Street. This was built in a French Renaissance style and was opened with great ceremony in 1887 and demolished in the late 1970s. The bakery was famous for its wedding cakes, many destined for admiration and consumption at the weddings in the nearby St Mungo's Co-operative Halls. The tenements built for the bakery workers — 'the last tenements in Hutchesontown' — still survive in good condition and occupied by families in Ballater Street, and can be recognised by the letters UCBS 1903 and the Co-operative Society's emblem, the clasped hand, on the stonework.

Hutchesontown (2); churches and schools

Hutchesontown Parish Church in Old Rutherglen Road has recently been demolished. This was the last remaining Church of Scotland in use in Hutchesontown, and included members of the former congregations of Augustine, Buchanan Memorial, Cumberland Street, Oatlands, St Bernard's and Shearer Memorial Churches. The only remaining Church of Scotland building is the shell of Alexander Thomson's Caledonia Road Church, which was built for a United Presbyterian congregation in 1857. The building was sold to Glasgow Corporation shortly after the congregation was dissolved in 1963, and soon after was destroyed by fire with the loss of the magnificent painted interior. Only the front wall with its pillars and its distinctive tower now remain intact. In 1989 there were plans to convert the church to a restaurant and function rooms, but the future of the A-listed building remains undecided.

The only remaining Roman Catholic Church in use in Hutchesontown is Blessed John Duns Scotus with its associated

Franciscan Friary in Ballater Street. The church was the former St Luke's which opened in 1975 and has a fine interior designed by the architect W Gilmour. Since 1993 the congregation has been formed from members of four local Catholic churches, St John the Evangelist, St Francis, St Bonaventure and St Luke. St Francis was opened by the Franciscan Order in 1868. The first building soon proved too small and a new church and friary were built on the same site in Cumberland Street by Pugin & Pugin between 1878-95. This fine building closed for worship in 1993. The church has good acoustics and was used at Mayfest 1995 for a production of *The Pied Piper of Hutchesontown*. The play chronicled the impact of 'Regeneration' on the community through the years, bringing together professional and amateur performers, and allowing the audience into the lives of Gorbals folk and laughing and crying with them. Among the memories stirred were the days when St Francis had its own pipe band dressed in their Macintosh tartan uniform. The friary is being made into 16 flats of amenity housing, and it is planned to convert the church for housing, St Bonaventure's and St John's are both now demolished.

The Southern Necropolis on the south side of Caledonia Road was first laid out in 1831 and was intended to be to Gorbals what the Necropolis was to Glasgow and Pere Lachaise was to Paris: a dignified and imposing place of rest for citizens of worth. The imposing gateway tower was built in 1848 to a design by Charles Wilson. Among those buried here are the millionaire grocer, Sir Thomas Lipton, who was born in Gorbals in 1850; Hugh Macdonald, the author of the popular *Rambles around Glasgow;* Charles Wilson and his fellow architect James Salmon. A meeting in 1839 decreed that the ground had been laid out 'to enable the working classes to become proprietors of burying places' and records show that this is also the resting place of cotton-workers, miners, soldiers, actors, musicians, engineers and industrialists. Much work in tidying the cemetery and researching records was carried out by the Gorbals Fair Committee History Group.

Educational returns made in 1834 stated that there was no parochial or burgh school in Gorbals parish, but four charity schools existed: one supported by the Parish church and the Relief Church; another by the Catholic Church; a third school by a charity and small fees; and the fourth a girls' school 'privately endowed by a lady'. The two last mentioned were probably the Gorbals

The architect David Hamilton recommended in 1841 that Hutchesons' Boys' School should be built in Crown Street 'for the quietness of the situation, good air and the roomy and open site'. In 1960 the school moved to a new site at Crossmyloof.

Youths' School in Greenside (later Cleland) Street, and Miss McFarlane's School in Surrey Street, A later report also mentions a school in Wellington Place provided by Neale Thomson for his mill workers.

As well as these well-run schools, there were many schools run for private venture, or profit. Thirty-five such schools were known to operate in Gorbals in 1834. When the Argyll Commission Inspectors visited one such 'adventure' school in a two-roomed house in Hutchesontown in the 1860s, their report read as follows:

> Both rooms were packed full of dirty ragged children, looking rosy through dirt, and evidently belonging to the very poorest families in the district. There were 47 present, and some of them accommodated in the kitchen-bed. The air was loaded with noxious smells, and it was a relief to escape into the open street. The education had no reality about it. There was all the buzz and fuss of a school, but there were no results.

In 1839 the patrons of Hutchesons' Hospital decided to erect a new purpose-built school on their lands in Hutchesontown. This was for the benefit of boys receiving their education through the benevolence of George and Thomas Hutcheson of Lambhill who had founded the school for the maintenance and education of twelve poor boys in 1641. The boys were at first accommodated with the 'poor, aiget, decrippit men' in Hutchesons' Hospital in the Trongate, but after a few years they were boarded out and assistance given for their clothing and keep. When the Hospital moved into new premises in Ingram Street in 1805, the top floor was intended for a schoolroom, but instead the scholars were given a small side room, which became increasingly inadequate as the roll rose to 120 by 1840. The distinguished architect, David Hamilton, recommended the new site in Crown Street as being 'by far the most appropriate and best in all respects, from the quietness of the situation, good air, roomy and open site, with good access from all directions'. The new school, opened on 26 April 1841, had three classrooms for 140 scholars. The boys attended school for four years, generally from the age of seven, were taught reading, writing and common arithmetic, and left as bound apprentices to different trades.

After 1872 entrance was no longer limited to Foundationers, moderate fees were charged and instruction was given up to University Entrance standard. The school was extended in the 1870s to accommodate 500 pupils by increasing the number of classrooms to eleven and adding a gymnasium and an assembly hall. At the same time a new central tower was erected with a belfry and a dome. This school remained in use until the school moved to Crossmyloof in 1960. A separate Hutchesons' Girls' School was opened in 1876 in Elgin Street and moved to new buildings in Kingarth Street in Strathbungo in 1912. In 1976 Hutchesons' Grammar School at Crossmyloof became coeducational and the Kingarth Street buildings are now the Junior School.

At present there are five primary schools in the Gorbals area: Abbotsford and St John's RC at Laurieston; Blackfriars and St Francis RC in Hutchesontown; and St Bonaventure RC in Oatlands to the east. In 1993 children from Blackfriars, accompanied by Head Teacher, Mrs Marjorie McLennan, went to St James's Palace to meet the Queen who presented them with the Queen's Anniversary Trust Award for the environment work the school carried out in their area of Gorbals. The former Adelphi Terrace Public School at the north end of Florence Street, built in 1894 by the Gorbals School Board, is now used as the Photography and Design Annexe of the Glasgow College of Building. The large white building on the river-front on the west side of the Albert Bridge is the Glasgow College of Nautical Studies, built in the 1960s and easily recognised from its domed planetarium, rooftop radar masts and the ship's mast facing towards the river.

The good folk of the Gorbals: Irish, Jews and Asians

The first of the immigrant groups to settle in the Gorbals were the Irish, who began to arrive in the early 19th century, and were often blamed for the overcrowding which occurred as ever more people poured into the area without provision for additional accommodation. It is worth noting the comment made in Edwin Chadwick's famous *Report on the Sanitary Condition of the Labouring Population of Great Britain* in 1842 that 'the bad name of the poor Irish had been too long attached to them' and that they appeared to exhibit 'much less of that squalid misery and addiction to the use of ardent spirits than the Scotch of the same grade'. Several noteworthy citizens of Glasgow were born in the Gorbals to Irish families: Tommy Lipton, whose parents came from Ulster and ran a grocer's shop in Crown Street; Benny Lynch, fly-weight champion of the world; Pat Crerand and Charlie Gallacher, who both made their name as footballers with Celtic. Lord Provost Patrick Lally, who took office in 1996, was born and raised in Thistle Street and has long represented the interest of the residents of Castlemilk, many of whom also have their roots in the Gorbals.

In 1831 there were only 47 Jews in Glasgow. These were mostly business men or merchants, mainly of German or Dutch origin, who settled north of the Clyde. By 1879 the numbers had increased sufficiently for the first purpose-built synagogue in Scotland to be built at Garnethill. The second large influx of Jews into Glasgow began in the 1880s, when refugees from Russia and Poland settled, unlike the earlier Jewish community, in the Gorbals. The first synagogue south of the Clyde was consecrated in 1880 in Commerce Street in Tradeston and in 1901 the Great Synagogue was opened in Laurieston at 93 South Portland Street, and remained the principal place of worship until closure in 1974. Other synagogues were the Chevra Kadisha (Holy Congregation) in Buchan Street and the Bes Hamedrash Hagadol (Great House of Study) first in Govan Road (Ballater Street) then from 1925–56 in the New Central Synagogue at the corner of Hospital Street and Rutherglen Road.

By 1885 more than half the pupils in Gorbals Primary School were Jewish and in 1895 a religious school for Jews was opened, the Talmud Torah, which boys attended after school hours.

Between the 1890s and 1914 the Jewish population in Glasgow increased from two to six thousand. Many Jews were small shop-keepers and this was the period when Yiddish names and signs were frequently to be seen in shop windows. For many years Mrs Sophie Geneen managed a well-known hotel and restaurant in Abbotsford Place, with Richard Tauber, Joe Loss and Larry Adler among her guests. Around 1890 about one thousand Jews in Glasgow were employed in tailoring, many by Arthur & Co, who recruited skilled Jewish workers in London. Many others were employed in the tobacco manufacturing firm of Stephen Mitchell & Sons, or by cabinet-makers such as Leon & Co of Ballater Street. The Elite Bedding Co, which is still in business in Commercial Road, is owned by the Weiss family. One of Gorbals most famous sons, Isaac Wolfson, born in Hospital Street, owned a cabinet-making business before taking control of Great Universal Stores, the largest mail order business in Britain The Jewish Institute next door to the Great Synagogue was the focal point of Jewish social life with facilities for athletics, a library, restaurant and splendid ball-room. The Oxford Star was a Jewish football team and the Jewish Lads' Brigade wore kilts and were the only all-Jewish pipe band in the world. The Jewish Institute Players were a talented company founded by Avron Greenbaum in 1936. Other Jews who lived in the Gorbals were Sir Monty Finnieston, former Chairman of British Steel, and the sculptor, Benno Schotz, whose native land was Estonia.

By the turn of the century some Jews had already moved out of the Gorbals to suburbs further south. In 1901 a Jewish society or 'Chevra' was formed in Govanhill and a Hebrew congregation was formed for Langside, Cathcart and Mount Florida areas in 1906. The main drift out of Gorbals took place between 1930 and 1955. The Jewish Institute moved to Pollokshields in 1970 and ten years later hardly a Jew was left in the Gorbals and not a single Jewish building now remains.

Fortunately the newspapers published by the Golombok family have survived: the *Jewish Voice*, a monthly paper published in Yiddish; and the *Jewish Echo*, which appeared weekly from 1928–1992.

Vivid pictures of Jewish life in the Gorbals can also be enjoyed

Jewish shops on the west side of Gorbals Street just south of Gorbals Cross, photographed in 1938. Mrs Sophie Geneen also ran a well-known hotel and restaurant in Abbotsford Place.

in novels such as Evelyn Cowan's *Spring Remembered*, Chaim Bermant's *Coming Home*, Ralph Glasser's *Growing up in the Gorbals* and in *The Scottish Shtetl*, edited by H Kaplan and C Hutt.

As the Jewish community moved out of the Gorbals, much of the area vacated was filled by Asian immigrants, Moslems from the West Punjab, now in Pakistan, and Hindus and Sikhs from the East Punjab, now in India. By 1940 the Moslem community was sufficiently large to set up a mission in a temporary mosque in Gorbals Street. The following year the Sikh Association acquired a temple in South Portland Street. Immigration accelerated in the late 1940s as wives and children began to arrive and families put down roots in Glasgow. Most men found employment as pedlars, or on public transport or opened small shops or retail outlets, and by the 1970s many Asian families were able to move to better accommodation in Govanhill, Pollokshields or suburbs further south. The large Central Mosque on the south bank of the Clyde was opened in May 1984 and is one of the largest in Europe and can take up to 1,500 worshippers. Its golden dome and slender minaret are now city landmarks. The mosque took five years to build and part of the £2.5m cost was met by donations from the Prince of Mecca and the Mayor of Jeddah and funds raised in other

Moslem countries as well as from the 15,000 strong Moslem community in Glasgow.

In *The New Scots: The Story of the Asians in Scotland*, Bashir Maan tells of the success story of Yaqub Ali, who came to Scotland in 1952 as an illiterate young man of 19 years with a couple of pounds in his pocket and by 1984 was a millionaire. Yaqub began as a pedlar, opened a drapery warehouse, learned English, then with his brother Taj founded A A Brothers and turned the business into a large chain of licensed grocers. He then turned the 24 acre Dixon's Blazes site into Europe's largest cash and carry warehouse, the Castle Cash & Carry. This was opened by Princess Anne in 1983 and a year later Mr Ali was awarded an OBE for his services to trade and industry. Mr Maan was himself Glasgow's first Asian councillor.

The Glasgow Citizens' Theatre

Three nights before Hogmanay 1878, the first theatre in the Gorbals, Her Majesty's, opened its doors in Main Street, just to the south of Gorbals Cross. The name was changed to the Royal Princess's two years later. In 1996 the same building is in use as the Glasgow Citizens' Theatre, although without its ornate frontage with Doric columns and a row of six statues on the parapet above, believed to have come originally from David Hamilton's Union Bank building in Ingram Street. The statues of the four muses are now confined behind plate glass in the entrance hall and Burns and Shakespeare have been relegated to the foyer. Under the management of Richard Waldon and Harry McKelvie the Royal Princess's was a highly successful theatre, famous for pantomimes such as *The Isle of Hokeypokey* and *On Board the Kleptomania* and great entertainers such as Tommy Lorne and George West. These shows are remembered for 'The Hing', a pithy conversation between two Glesca wives from one Dress Circle box to the other.

The Citizens' Theatre came into being in 1943 through the initiative of the playwright James Bridie, whose ambition was to establish a fully professional Scottish National Theatre to show the works of Scottish authors and the pick of world drama. The first production was Bridie's *Holy Isle*, given in the Athenaeum Theatre, which was the Company's home for the first two years. Then followed memorable productions such as Alexander Reid's *The Lass wi' the Muckle Mou*, *Let Wives Tak Tent*, which was Moliere in the unique Robert Kemp style, and Albert Finney in Pirandello's

The revamped Citizens' Theatre during Mayfest 1996. Originally the Royal Princess's, famous for its pantomimes, the theatre became the Citizens' in 1945. The former ornate façade disappeared in the 1970s.

Henry IV. Several of the Citizens' actors joined the company from the Glasgow Unity Theatre. The Unity was formed in 1941 from five amateur groups with the intention of playing to working class audiences, but it was short-lived and closed in 1947. In its last season, when the Citizens' was producing Ibsen's *The Wild Duck* and Robert McLellan's *Jamie the Saxt*, the Unity was touring Britain with Robert McLeish's *The Gorbals Story*, perpetuating the disparaging image of Glasgow created in the 1930s through the novel *No Mean City*, written by Alexander McArthur, a Gorbals barber, with the assistance of a London journalist. Arthur Bliss's ballet *Miracle in the Gorbals* was also performed in 1946.

The Citizens' took a new direction in 1969 with the arrival of Giles Havergal as artistic director. His first production, an all-male Hamlet, brought a strong reaction. 'There were boos, cheers, hisses at the end — but no one went to sleep'. Another innovation was the opening of the Close Theatre Club by the Citizens' Company in a converted dance hall and casino next door. From 1965, until destroyed by fire in 1973, this was a venue for smaller productions, theatre workshops, late night films and poetry readings. As part

*Duncan Macrae as King James and Mollie Urquhart as Mistress Edward
in the Citizens' production of Robert McLellan's* Jamie the Saxt *in 1947.
The story of King James's 'journey' from low cunning to wisdom.*

of Mayfest 1995 and 1996 the Citizens' performed its own version
of *Swing Hammer Swing*, an adaptation of Jeff Torrington's prize-
winning novel, described as a portrait of the 'endangered Gorbals
community circa 1968'.

In this heart of Gorbals theatre-land there was also the Palace
Music Hall, which stood immediately to the right of the Royal
Princess's. The Palace operated as a variety theatre from 1904 to
1914, then as a cinema and latterly as a Bingo Hall until sudden
demolition in 1977. Over in the west-end of Gorbals, in Eglinton
Street, was the prestigious Coliseum Theatre, which opened in
1905 as the Clyde Music Hall. The building was designed by the
renowned theatre architect, Frank Matcham, and could seat 2,900
with another 300 standing. It was the scene of Glasgow's biggest
theatre riot when Dr Walford Bodie MD hung, outside the theatre,
crutches used by people he claimed to have cured by hypnotism
and electrical wonders, and was pelted by medical students
throwing eggs, tomatoes and oranges. Bodie claimed that MD
stood for 'Merry Devil'. James Bridie, under his own name of

Osborne Henry Mavor, was one of the students who received a small fine. The Coliseum operated from 1929–69 as a cinema, beginning with a showing of Glasgow's first 'talkie', Al Johnson's *The Singing Fool*. Near the Coliseum is the New Bedford cinema, a 1932 building with an Art Deco facade. Both buildings are now Bingo Halls.

The Regeneration of Gorbals: the way forward

In 1957 Glasgow was again seized by a 'dinging-doun' fever. This time it took the form of an outbreak of CDAs, Comprehensive Development Areas, which indiscriminately swept away all before them with the virulence of a medieval plague. Three areas were designated in Gorbals: Hutchesontown-Gorbals, Laurieston-Gorbals, and Oatlands and Polmadie. The plan for Hutchesontown-Gorbals, east of Gorbals Street, was approved in 1957 and five schemes were completed by 1970. Robert Matthew and Basil Spence were appointed design consultants to A G Jury, the City Architect and Planner. The first scheme was the three and four room maisonettes opposite Queen Elizabeth Square, built by the SSHA. These were followed by Hutchesontown B, a mixed development on the banks of the Clyde in the Waddell Street area, consisting of four 17-storey blocks and lower buildings designed by Matthew and completed in 1963. Hutchesontown C, completed in 1965, was a mixture of housing and shops at Queen Elizabeth Square. This included two tower blocks designed by Spence containing 400 maisonettes which had to be demolished in 1993 because the flats were unattractive to tenants and would have cost £15–20m for improvement. Unfortunately the demolition was not properly carried out and resulted in the death of Mrs Helen Tinney, who was struck by masonry. Hutchesontown E at Crown Street, opened by the Queen in 1969, had an even shorter life, as 756 deck-access flats had to be demolished in 1987 because of dampness problems. Two tower blocks, the Sandieland Flats on the west side of Crown Street, are the sole survivors of 'Hutchie E'.

This was the Gorbals of Adam McNaughtan's ballad, popularly known as the *Jeely Piece Song:*

Oh, ye canny fling pieces oot a twenty storey flat
Seven hundred hungry weans will testify to that
If its butter, cheese or jeely, if the breid is plain or pan
The odds against it reachin' us is ninety nine tae wan.

Waiting for a turn on a swing, or watching for a 'jeely piece' flung out of a twenty-storey flat? Residents of the high flats enjoy a Gorbals play-park in the hot summer of 1995.

The much smaller Laurieston-Gorbals CDA was designated in 1965, by which time housing policy was changing in favour of refurbishing old tenement property. By this time, however, there were almost no tenements left to refurbish. One sole tenement has been retained in Gorbals Street as an A listed building, but is empty and forlorn-looking. In the third CDA at Polmadie the tenements were largely retained and improved.

By 1984 only 12,000 people were left in the Gorbals, compared to 85,000 in 1931 and 68,000 in 1951. The result was loss of shopping, educational and leisure facilities. In 1994 the Crown Street Regeneration Project was inaugurated with the aim of attracting people back to live in Gorbals in a mixture of rented and privately owned accommodation, built mainly on the site of the old 'Hutchie E' flats. The first phase, Ballater Gardens between Ballater Street and Old Rutherglen Road, is now complete and includes the houses at Benny Lynch Court, called after the world-champion fly-weight boxer, who was born in Florence Street, over which many of the houses are built. New developments are

View from Crown Street along Old Rutherglen Road, showing a variety of housing styles in the new 'Gorbals Village'. In the background the roof of an old cotton mill renovated as a business centre.

underway at Errol Gardens and Cumberland Gardens, and also planned are a park, a hotel and student accommodation. Elsewhere in Gorbals the West of Scotland Housing Association and the YMCA Housing Association have both built single persons' housing, and the Salvation Army have built a hostel for homeless persons in Oxford Street. A lottery grant will meet about one-third of the £6.3m cost of building a long-overdue leisure centre, including a replacement for Gorbals Baths, closed in 1981. These are the beginnings of the new 'Gorbals Village' which will take this ancient community forward into the 21st century.

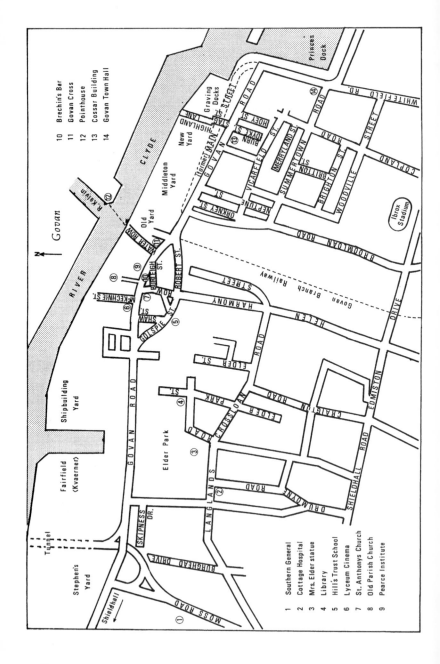

Govan

CLYDE

RIVER

Shipbuilding Yard

Fairfield (Kvaerner)

Stephen's Yard

Tunnel

Shieldhall

Southern General

1   Southern General
2   Cottage Hospital
3   Mrs. Elder statue
4   Library
5   Hill's Trust School
6   Lyceum Cinema
7   St. Anthonys Church
8   Old Parish Church
9   Pearce Institute

10   Brechin's Bar
11   Govan Cross
12   Pointhouse
13   Cossar Building
14   Govan Town Hall

New Yard

Middleton Yard

Old Yard

Graving Docks

Princes Dock

Ibrox Stadium

GOVAN ROAD

LANGLANDS ROAD

Elder Park

ELDER ST.

ELDER ST.

CROSSLOAN ROAD

DRUMOYNE ROAD

SHIELDHALL ROAD

CHARLTON ROAD

EDMISTON DRIVE

HARMONY STREET

HELEN ST.

BROOMLOAN ROAD

Govan Branch Railway

PARK ST.

SUMMERTOWN RD.

VICARFIELD ST.

NEPTUNE ST.

ORKNEY ST.

BRITTON ST.

BRIGHTON ST.

WOODVILLE ST.

MERRYLAND ST.

COPLAND RD.

WHITEFIELD RD.

GOVAN ROAD

HIGHLAND LANE

Thorter LANE

MAIN STREET

BURNT ST.

DYKE ST.

HOEY ST.

SHAW ST.

BURLEIGH ST.

ROBERT ST.

WATER ROW

McKECHNIE ST.

GOVAN ROAD

SKIPNESS DR.

BURGHEAD DRIVE

MOSS ROAD

R. Kelvin

74

CHAPTER 4
GOVAN

Meikle Govan: a gret and ane large village

Govan is situated on the south bank of the river Clyde, opposite the mouth of the Kelvin. By the 10th century, an important ecclesiastical establishment was in existence, and in medieval times Govan lay at the centre of an extensive parish which stretched to Polmadie on the east and Kelvinside in the north. An old route, Water Row, led down to a ford, and from the 16th century on, a ferry plied across the river to Pointhouse near Partick in the northern part of the parish. The first known reference to Govan in written documents dates back to 1134 when King David I granted Govan to the church of Glasgow. Floods are mentioned at Govan in 1454 when 'ane richt gret speit in Clyd...put all the toune of Govane in ane flot, quile the folks sat on the housis'.

By the 16th century there was, according to Bishop Leslie, 'a gret and ane large village upon the water of Clyd named Govan whare ale is wondrous guid'. The village was known as 'Meikle Govan' — large Govan — to distinguish it from 'Little Govan' or Gorbals. It appears as 'Mekle Govan' on Pont's map surveyed in the 1590s. The names of some early residents of Meikle Govan are known from the Rental Book of the Archbishop of Glasgow in the time of Mary Queen of Scots. In 1546 Thom and Jhon Gybson appear in the weyst end of Mekle Govan, and Wilzam Anderson and Bessy Hardy his wef in eyst ende of Mykle Gowan; in 1557 Jhone Clwne in land of the west end of Gowan callit Tewichirhill quarter, and Robert Lieche in the quarter callit Dwmbrek. Other names appearing in Meikle Govan in the 1560s are Rankin, Rowain, Cutbert, Paterson and Barnat.

Because of the break-up of church lands into small portions after the Reformation, the Govan area had no large land-owners, but 'gentlemen's residences' sprang up as Glaswegians moved out of the increasingly crowded city. Richardson's map of 1795 shows some such houses with their owners' names: Shieldhall (Alex. Oswald), Linthouse (Spreul Shortridge), Fairfield (John Cumming), Holmfauldhead (Steven Rowand), Merryflats (Peter Paterson),

An aerial view of Govan around 1935, looking down-river. On the left bank Harland & Wolff's shipyard, Govan Old Parish Church, Govan Cross and Water Row. Across the river, D & W Henderson's shipyard at Meadowside.

Greenhead (Good) and Broomloan (R. Ronald). Other houses appear on the Ordnance Survey map of 1859, surrounded by their gardens and ornamental grounds: Whitefield House, Vicarfield House, Moore Park, Ibroxholm and Harmony House. Many have survived as street names, along with the names of old farms: Greenfield, Langlands, Moss and Drumoyne.

The village took shape along the old road from Glasgow to Renfrew and in 1793 it contained over 200 families. A Weavers' Society had been in existence from 1756 and played an important part in the history of the village. Because the Clyde at Govan was shallow and sluggish, and there were no fast-flowing tributaries in the area to provide water-power, Govan escaped the bleach-fields, extensive dyeworks and large cotton mills which transformed other small communities in the early 19th century and blighted the countryside. Before 1840 the only industry was a small dyeworks just east of Water Row and a silk mill at the west end of the village. Handloom weaving was still the principal occupation in the 1840s.

The arrival of shipbuilding in 1839 brought only a slow increase in population until mid-century, after which the population of Govan expanded at a rate almost unmatched in Scotland, from around 9,000 in 1864 when Govan became a Burgh to 91,000 in 1912 when it was taken into Glasgow. First tenements, then council housing schemes, covered the estates and farmland. With the decline of shipbuilding in the 1960s, a fall in population, and the decay of 19th-century housing, Govan became one of the earliest of the city's Comprehensive Development Areas in 1969. Fortunately many public buildings erected at the height of Govan's prosperity have been saved and improved, and the riverside is being regenerated with a mixture of attractive public and private housing which will take Govan into yet another century of its long and distinguished history.

Govan Old Parish Church

Govan Old Parish Church is situated just west of Water Row. The church is modern, completed by Robert Rowand Anderson in 1888, but the site is of great antiquity. The size and shape of the curvilinear enclosure round the graveyard are an indication that Govan was an important early ecclesiastical centre, but only minor excavations have been carried out and the date of the earliest church remains speculative. The present church is at least the fourth on the site.

Although tradition says that Govan was the burial place of a 6th century King Constantine of Cornwall, it is now thought more likely that Govan became an important cult centre about the mid-9th century and as such served as a burial place for wealthy patrons for around 200 years. The name of St Constantine may have attached itself to the site through associations with one of the several Constantines of the increasingly powerful kingdom of Dalriada: perhaps the son of Kenneth mac Alpin, Constantine I, killed in battle against the Norse in 879; or an earlier Constantine, who founded the church of Dunkeld and died around 820. The church could be seen as a minster from which priests went out to serve dependent churches, perhaps even the temporary seat of a bishop, ministering to a community of mixed origins.

The hoard of sculptured tombstones uncovered by the beadle digging a grave in Govan churchyard in 1855 is now recognised as one of the most remarkable assemblages of early medieval

A drawing by Chalmers of the front of the sarcophagus discovered in Govan churchyard in 1855. The carvings depict a stag pursued by a huntsman, and a backward-facing beast trampling another beast and a serpent.

sculpture in Scotland. None is considered earlier than mid-ninth century. A number of stones were damaged or destroyed when the Harland & Wolff platers' shed adjacent to the east wall of the graveyard was demolished in 1973. All 31 remaining stones have been moved into the church with the exception of one large stone. The outstanding item in the collection, the richly ornamented sarcophagus, the sole survivor of three reported existing in the churchyard in 1762, had already been transferred to the chancel of the church in 1905 and 'lifted by the strength of ten men' on to a specially designed stone table bearing the inscription:

> The reputed shrine of St Constantine K. and M. founder of Govan Church A.D., 576. Preserved within the ancient church. Buried in the churchyard A.D., 1762. Discovered A.D., 1855.

The sarcophagus is a full-length, free-standing, stone shrine-coffin. The lid is missing. It is carved on four sides with panels of interlacing and panels depicting a horseman armed with a short sword hunting a stag, the Lamb of God driving back the serpent, and on the back, strange beasts facing away from each other.

Most of the stones are grave-slabs, which lay flat on the ground to mark a grave, but the collection includes four upright stones, carved on both sides. One of these has a carving of a rider astride a remarkably docile horse, locally known as the 'Cuddy Stane', and is possibly an early representation of Christ riding into Jerusalem on Palm Sunday on a donkey. A second cross-slab is known as the 'Sun Stone'. This has the customary carved cross and interlacing on one side and on the other, three snake-like bodies spiralling out of a central boss as though it is spinning clockwise. The other two upright stones are the Jordanhill Cross and the Govan Cross, of which only the shafts remain. A scene on one side of the Govan Cross may depict the anointing of David by Samuel. The collection is completed by five hogback stones, displayed in the transept, monuments to the Vikings who had settled in the area by the 10th century. The Govan group of hogbacks are distinctive because of their massive size.

Shortly after King David gave Govan to the Church of Glasgow, Govan became a prebend of Glasgow Cathedral. After the Reformation the teinds of Govan were granted to the University of Glasgow and the Principal of the University was appointed Minister of the Parish and required to preach at Govan every Sunday. The last of the four principals to discharge his duties at Govan was the Presbyterian reformer, Andrew Melville, who left for St Andrews in 1580, after which Govan had its own ministers, the first being Thomas Smeaton. Among his twenty-four successors was Dr John Macleod, in whose time the present church was built, and who planned the stained glass windows executed by Charles Kempe. Dr George Fielden MacLeod, later Lord MacLeod of Fuinary, came as minister to Govan in the 1930s and became known for his work among the unemployed. Although awarded the Military Cross in the First World War, he later became a committed pacifist, and left Govan in 1938 to found the Iona Community, which still has its headquarters in the Pearce Institute. In May 1991 Lord MacLeod was given the Freedom of the City of Glasgow by Lord Provost Susan Baird. He died later the same year at the age of 96. The present minister of Govan Old is the Rev T A Davidson Kelly.

East-enders, West-enders, Water Row, the Golly and the Gravey

In 1793 the Rev John Pollock reported that there were 224 families in the village of Govan where, regrettably, neither cleanliness nor godliness was conspicuous. The old houses were in general ill aired, incommodious and dirty. Stagnant water on either side of the public road through the village (about a mile in length) was until recently 'highly offensive to travellers'. And yet, 'though the effluvia arising from it could not be of a salubrious quality', the people were generally exceedingly healthy, and many of them reached a very advanced age. There was no local baker, butcher or public market. Loaf bread sent from Glasgow was underweight, coal was overcharged, and there was no civil magistrate to enforce the laws and punish crimes. Among the operative people, including the weavers, 'temperance, it is much to be lamented, has not obtained a place among the cardinal virtues'. Mr Pollock demands action to mend the churchyard gate and wall 'to prevent the burying-ground from being indecently used like a common thoroughfare and place of diversion'. From other reports it appears that cattle were pastured in the churchyard.

From earliest times Govan was divided into an 'East End' and a 'West End' with Govan Cross and Water Row as the dividing line. The *Transactions* of the Old Govan Club, published in the first decades of this century, contain many nostalgic reminiscences of the different parts of Govan in the last part of the 19th century. The main part of the village was the east end, with a cluster of single storey cottages extending along Main Street from Whitefield Road to the Cross. Main Street ran in crescent shape a little to the north of the present Govan Road, on the line of Clydebrae Street. Near the east end of the town, Stag Street and its continuation Highland Lane, led down to the river where a ferry crossed to Yorkhill. This was a very old route, where Highland drovers once crossed the Clyde with their cattle on their way to southern markets. There was a right of way along the river bank from Highland Lane to Water Row. The first shipyards were built along this stretch of river in the 1840s.

By the 1850s there were very good grocery and provision shops along Main Street. The principal taverns were the Sheephead and the Black Bull at the end nearest the Cross, and the Stag Inn at the east end. From 1843 there was a Free Church and school, but expansion of the shipyards forced the congregation to move across Govan Road to a new church at Summertown in 1873. The vacated church then became the Clyde Music Halls. The name was later changed to the Royal Prince's Theatre, where a versatile company performed *Hamlet, Othello, Shamus O'Brien* or any other tragedy or farce. But 'the better classes shunned it, and it came to grief', becoming a horse feeding store, then a Salvation Army Citadel, and finally, along with much of the Auld Toun, made way for the graving docks at the turn of the century.

Much lore surrounded the inn at Water Row. A 16th-century feu grant has 'John McNair in Ferrie Bot of the 12s 6d land there' along with Jonet Dunlop, his wife. King James V, disguised as the

The village of Govan in the 1840s drawn by Thomas Fairbairn. The church spire is a copy of that of Stratford-upon-Avon, and belonged to a former parish church built in 1826.

'Guid Man of Ballengeich' is said to have spent 'blythesome nights' here with the curate of Govan. In the Rev Mr Pollock's time the inn was kept by a shrewd, pawky and witty individual called David Dreghorn, and was the rendezvous for the monthly meeting of the 'White Wine Club'. Here some of Glasgow's notable gentlemen could eat salmon caught under the windows of the hostelry and freely quaff Scotland's 'vin blanc' as they liked to refer to their whisky. The inn later became Buchanan's Waverley tavern, where good hot meat pies and porter could be had on Saturday afternoons and nights. A descendant of the owner of the 'Buc' transferred the licence around 1900 to Langlands Road.

A small dyeworks was begun around 1824 by Alexander Reid at the east side of Water Row near a berth where smacks coming from the Gareloch and Loch Lomond could unload their cargoes of timber. Reid's works 'perfumed the air with the bitter tang of the oak which made one regard the scent almost as a taste'. The water supply came from a reservoir twelve feet deep on top of an artificial mound known locally as 'Doomster Hill', When the pond was deepened, fragments of bones were found, suggesting that this may have been a pre-Christian burial mound. The hillock may also have served as a law-hill, from where the 'Dempster' may have pronounced judgement and sentence.

The west end of Meikle Govan consisted of a few scattered houses facing the old kirk and extending as far west as Shaw Street. The people of this part of town were known as the 'West-enders', and spoke condescendingly of the 'East-enders' as 'in the ither end o' the toon, puir buddies'. The East-enders retaliated with 'thae wad-be gairdner cratters wast o' the Cross'. This was a jibe at Govan West's reputation as a producer of the ubiquitous 'grossets' so beloved of ramblers from Glasgow, Just to the west of the Cross was a row of cottages called Oakum Bay. These stretched along Govan Road where Brechin's Bar now stands at the corner of Burleigh Street, and were occupied by workers who prepared the oakum for caulking the seams of the wooden decks of ships. Next came the Wheatsheaf Inn and a smithy before reaching the 'Big Loan', now Harmony Row. The Loan led to Harmony House, a mansion with a large garden. Langlands Road was known as the 'Wee Loan' and Burleigh Street as the 'Old Causeway'.

The triangular area formed by these three old streets became known as the 'Golly', although on a map drawn in 1837, this name is attached to Harmony Row only. The 'Golly' or 'Goalie' is said to be named after a John Galt, the proprietor of 'Galt's Land', a local builder credited with erecting the churches of St Anthony's, St Mary's, and Copland Road UP. Facing the 'Golly' immediately across Govan Road is the 'Gravey', the territory round the old graveyard. Shaw Street at the west end of the village was a very short street, with a kind of square on the corner with Govan Road. This was the Kittle Corner, 'kittle' meaning awkward, or twisting. Despite its reputation as a cold, draughty, inhospitable place, this seems to have been a favourite street-corner meeting place for the West End worthies. Another sharp corner nearby was known as the 'Deil's Elbow'.

Just beyond the village was the silk mill erected by Morris Pollok for the throwing (ie spinning) of silk, claimed as the first such factory in Scotland. It stood near the river on ground later occupied by Fairfield shipyard and was considered romantic enough to appear in an engraving by Swan in 1824. Mr Pollok was 'a stately gentleman' who always wore a tall hat and a blue coat. He lived in Govan Mansion House beside the factory, and every morning went out to the fish pond in his garden and fed the fishes. The larger proportion of his 250 employees in 1839 were

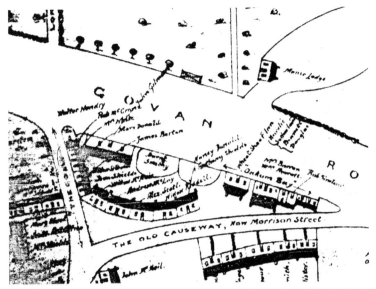

Part of a map of The Village of Govan, 1837, *drawn by W D Barles in 1906. This area is still known locally as 'The Golly' after John Galt, a local builder. The map places the name 'Golly' on the north part of Harmony Row, between the Old Causeway (later Morrison Street and now Burleigh Street) and Govan Road.*

children from eight years upwards, working a ten hour day, but a novel warm air system ensured the 'total absence of that feeling of suffocation met with in most other factories'. The mill closed shortly after 1873 because of a serious fire and increased competition, but remained a landmark for shipping until demolished in 1901, to make way for an extension to the Fairfield yard.

The Shipbuilders I

> We slowly passed
> Loud building yards, where every slip contained
> A mighty vessel, with a hundred men
> Battering its iron sides.

Shipbuilding was begun at Govan in 1839 by Macarthur and Alexander on ground just to the east of Water Row, on the site previously occupied by 'Doomster Hill'. The 'Old Yard' was always held in great affection by Govanites as the cradle of their great industry. The yard was taken over by Robert Napier two years later and after several other changes of ownership was occupied by Mackie and Thomson from 1889–1912. The second yard was the Middleton Iron Ship Building Yard, started a little way upriver by Smith and Rodger, who in 1844 built the paddle steamers *Caledonia* and *Edinburgh Castle*. This yard was taken over twenty years later by the London and Glasgow Shipbuilding & Engineering Company Limited. Immediately to the east of the 'Limited', as the yard was always known, Robert Napier opened another yard 'Govan East Iron Ship Building Yard' in 1850. The 'New Yard' worked simultaneously with the 'Old Yard' until the latter was sold in 1858 to Randolph and Elder. Napier was primarily a marine engineer, at first fitting engines into hulls built elsewhere. After his move downriver from Lancefield to Govan, he turned his attention to building his own iron steamships, beginning with *Vanguard* in 1843. During the Crimean War Napier built iron-clad warships for the Admiralty, the best known being the *Black Prince,* launched with much ceremony in 1862. After Napier's death in 1876, the business was acquired by Alexander Kirk, who (while still at Fairfield) had designed the important marine triple expansion engine.

In 1912 these three yards all came under the control of the Belfast shipbuilders, Harland & Wolff. The managing director, Lord Pirrie, formed the three yards into one, beginning by laying out new berths and a fitting-out basin. The yard closed in 1962. The former Harland & Wolff engine shed, nearly the size of a football pitch, was turned into a venue for the play, *The Ship*, one of the highlights of the 1990 City of Culture celebrations. Another epic, the *Big Picnic*, was staged in The Shed in 1994 and told the story of Glasgow soldiers who went to the front during the First World War.

The early workforce in the shipyards lived in the Auld Toun, but by the 1860s families were beginning to move to the new tenements on the south side of Govan Road. The first rows of tenements were built in Alma (now Hoey) Street, Albert (now Orkney) and Victoria (now Neptune) streets. Villas were built in Windsor Street, Brighton Street, Buckingham Terrace and Osborne Terrace. The names were chosen to commemorate the British victories in the Crimean War, the monarchy and the royal residences. All Govan had turned out to greet the Queen, her Consort and the Prince of Wales as they sailed up the Clyde for the royal visit to Glasgow in 1859, and had not Govan men built the great iron-clads for the British navy? Alma Street was one of the first streets in New Govan, and was considered one of the most respectable, where the foremen in the yards lived.

A considerable number of men from the West Highlands were working in the yards in the 1850s: mostly men in their twenties, from Skye, Mull, Gigha, Morven, Knapdale and other parts of mainland Argyll, employed as iron shipbuilders, boilermakers, blacksmiths and labourers. A chapel was built in Burndyke Street in 1866 for the Gaelic-speaking community under the leadership of elders from St Columba's Church of Scotland in Glasgow. The church became St Kiaran's Parish Church in 1884. The Free Church also began Gaelic services in 1862 and in 1877 they built St Columba's Free Church, with Allan Cameron as the first minister. Part of that congregation continues today as St Columba's Free Church of Scotland in Britton Street.

Much of the ground occupied by these three yards is now covered by the houses at Napier Road, Terrace, Place and Drive, built in the 1970s as the Riverside Housing Scheme, Phase I, and fittingly named after the 'Father of Clyde Shipbuilding'.

The Shipbuilders II

Another famous shipbuilding firm began in 1852 when Charles Randolph and John Elder formed a partnership and worked together to develop an improved compound engine. Two years later the new engine was successfully fitted into the *Brandon,* reducing the rate of coal consumed per indicated horsepower from about $4^1/_2$lbs to $3^1/_4$lbs, a significant saving on long ocean voyages. Both men had served apprenticeships with Robert Napier, Randolph as a wright and Elder as an engineer. They next moved into shipbuilding, buying over Napier's 'Old Yard' in 1860, then opening new and extensive premises on the lands of Fairfield on the west side of Govan four years later. Their combined talents established a yard that has been continuously building ships for over 130 years.

One of the yard's first commissions was to build four fast ships for the Confederate States of America to run the Union blockade of the Southern ports. The fastest and the most notorious, was the *Falcon*. Randolph retired in 1868 and Elder died the year after at the early age of 45 years. The firm was then run by William Pearce and the name changed to Fairfield Shipbuilding and Engineering Company Ltd. Pearce had trained as a shipbuilder at the Royal Naval College in Chatham and combined engineering expertise with business acumen. Under his management the firm led the building of fast Atlantic liners — the 'greyhounds of the Atlantic' and reduced the crossing to six days, although Pearce never achieved his ambition of building a ship which would do the crossing in five days. The idea of the 'Blue Riband', an award for the fastest Atlantic crossing, came from Pearce and was won by two of his ships, the *Umbria* and the *Etruria*. The yard also built the curious circular steam-yacht *Livadia* for the Czar of Russia: a ship with three funnels abreast and five masts arranged one at each end and one in the middle; designed to be perfectly stable; a 'water palace' fitted out with a rose garden, illuminated fountains and wine racks for 10,000 bottles; a ship as never seen on Clyde before or since. *Livadia* survived storms in the Bay of Biscay and the Mediterranean and arrived in Sebastopol in better condition than the distinguished passengers, only to find on arrival that the Czar had been assassinated.

The Fairfield yard was designed to build not only large passenger and cargo ships, but also warships. These included *HMS Valiant* and *HMS Renown* in the First World War. During the Second World War Fairfield built 30 ships including the battleship *Howe* and the aircraft carrier *Implacable*, with a complement of 2,000 men and over 60 aeroplanes, as well as 16 landing craft and stocks of replacement engines. In 1968 the yard was merged into the unsuccessful Upper Clyde Shipbuilders Ltd. Four years later it reappeared as part of Govan Shipbuilders along with Stephen's and Connell's, but only after the workers staged a determined 14 month long work-in. Nationalisation followed in 1977, then the yard was sold to its present owners, the Norwegian firm Kvaerner, in 1988.

The last of the great Govan yards was Alexander Stephen & Sons, who moved across the Clyde from Kelvinhaugh in 1869 and started a new yard at Linthouse on the west of Govan. Stephen's are remembered for the banana boats they built for the West Indian trade and for the many naval craft they built during the Second World War, including *HMS Amethyst* which made the historic escape down the Yangtse river in 1949. Stephen's was merged into UCS and closed in 1970. The former yard is now occupied by Barr

The entrance to the main office of the Fairfield Shipyard, now Kvaerner Govan Ltd. The figures represent a shipwright and an engineer.

& Stroud, now a subsidiary of Pilkington Glass, who manufacture defence equipment in a new purpose built factory.

Many of the workers at Fairfield and Linthouse appear to have come to Govan in the 1860s from the traditional ship building centres on the east coast of Scotland: ship carpenters from Leith, Kincardine, Dundee, Aberdeen, Peterhead, Clachnaharry; or from centres in the south-west such as Portpatrick and Gatehouse. Ship riggers brought their specialist skills to Govan from Greenock, Port Glasgow and Montrose. To house the workforce, tenement building began in 1866 at Greenfield, with Helen Street and Robert Street set out in the same year. In 1864, when Randolph and Elder opened their yard, the population of Govan was 9,000. Only seven years later, the number had more than doubled to 19,000. The picture of Govan in 1871 is of a community transformed, enriched and invigorated by an influx of workers of diverse skills and mixed origins.

Isabella Elder: she lived in Glasgow, but her heart was in Govan

In 1857 John Elder married Isabella Ure and the couple set up house at 6 Claremont Terrace in the Park district of Glasgow. Isabella Ure was the daughter of Alexander Ure, a Glasgow solicitor. In the years following the death of her husband in 1869, Mrs Elder made generous gifts designed to improve the quality of education, health and recreation of the people of Glasgow and Govan. In 1871 she gave an additional endowment to the Chair of Civil Engineering at the University of Glasgow, and in 1883, a particularly generous year, she endowed the John Elder Chair of Naval Architecture and founded the Queen Margaret College for the higher education of women. Isabella Elder was awarded an honorary LL.B from the University in 1901. In 1883 Mrs Elder also turned her attention to Govan and purchased 36 acres of ground on the opposite side of Govan Road from the Fairfield shipyard and laid it out as a public park. She erected a bronze statue in memory of her husband, who stands with his hand resting gently on a compound engine, looking over to the great yard which he helped create. From the deed of gift, the park was to provide the inhabitants of burgh with 'healthful recreation by music and amusement'. An annual event in Govan was Mrs Elder's fireworks display in the park. The Salvation Army, and the SCWS and Govan Brass Bands all gave concerts from an octagonal cast-iron bandstand until it was pulled down one day during the last war by a lorry and a length of rope, presumably for scrap metal. Mrs Elder's last gifts to Govan were the Elderpark Library in a corner of the park and money for the building of the Elder Cottage Hospital and Training Houses for the Cottage Nurses, on the corner of Langlands Road and Drumoyne Road. The Elder family later gifted the David Elder Infirmary, now closed.

The ceremonies associated with Mrs Elder's gifts to Govan took place with much Victorian pomp and formality. The day of the opening of the park, 27 June 1885, was declared a public holiday, with trades and schools processions, a public address to Mrs Elder and a banquet in the Burgh Hall. The ceremony was performed by the Earl of Rosebery. The Marquis of Lothian unveiled the statue of John Elder on 28 July 1888, after the Prince of Wales, in Glasgow to make arrangements for the Queen's forthcoming visit to the

The statue of Mrs John Elder in a corner of the Elder Park which was one of her many gifts to the people of Govan. Isabella Elder wears the LL.B robes of the University of Glasgow, who granted her an Honorary degree.

International Exhibition, declined the invitation and by so doing, missed the downpour of rain which fell incessantly from morning to night. The Elderpark Library was opened by Andrew Carnegie. Mrs Elder died in 1905 in her 78th year. The following year a bronze statue in her memory, seated and wearing her LL.B robes, was unveiled in its own small enclosure in the park by the Duchess of Montrose.

Isabella Elder was also a woman ahead of her time, banning smoking at the opening ceremony of the park, insisting that the library should open on Sundays, and providing women with the chance of higher education. But she was also a realist, and her work in arranging classes for cookery, hygiene, darning and mending and especially budgeting for women and girls in Govan deserves to be better known. These efforts attracted the attention of the American consul in Glasgow, Mr Underwood, who sent back a report to the States in 1888 on 'Cookery for working men's wives', pointing out that 'the novelty consists in cheapness' and that he had seen a good palatable and nutritious meal for six people produced at a cost of a shilling (24 cents):

> There were produced some excellent dishes; fish soup, a kidney and liver soup, and a meat pie were the most successful. The fish soup was made of large cod heads with the addition of rice, onions and potatoes. The meat pie is called 'sea pie' because it is in general use among sailors. The peculiar excellence of Miss Gordon's method is making the meat tender and the crust light and not greasy.

Mrs Elder's school was reported in scientific and medical journals in Britain and Germany and thanks to Consul Underwood, the idea was taken up in the States and 'there was not a city in that vast country that he had visited that had not heard of Govan and Mrs Elder'.

The Burgh Years: 1864–1912

When Govan was a burgh and at the height of its prosperity, many fine public buildings were erected, and fortunately a good number have survived. These include the original Burgh Chambers in Orkney Street, now the Govan Police Station, and the large and impressive Town Hall built in 1901 in Govan Road. Also on Govan Road are the former Glasgow Savings Bank building of 1906, now occupied by the Trustee Savings Bank, and the *Govan Press* building of 1890. The *Govan Press* was published every Friday from 1878–1968 first by John Cossar, and after his death by his widow and son. On the facade are the heads of Gutenberg and Claxton, Walter Scott and Robert Burns, and John and Jane Cossar.

At Govan Cross the British Linen Bank building of 1900, surmounted by a handsome open crown, is now occupied by the Bank of Scotland. Over the entrance is a carved ship blown by winged wind gods, and between the windows can be seen tiny workmen such as bee-keepers, navigators and fishermen, perhaps symbolic of the Burgh motto 'Nihil sine Labore', nothing without work. Govan New Church on the east side of the square was begun in 1873 as part of the Free Church extension movement, and was known as St Mary's until 1982. Govan New is now a union of several congregations. The interior of the church is of unusual design, with no seat further than ten rows from the front. The cast-iron fountain in the centre of the square was erected in 1884 by the people of Govan in memory of Dr John Aitken, the much respected first medical officer of the burgh. Dr Aitken's assistant was Dr Barras, who thought that the vogue for holidaying 'doon the watter' was a symptom of 'neurotic unrest' and sent patients instead to 'Craw Jock's' at Dumbreck for cream and milk and Abernethy biscuits. Behind the Cross in Water Row is now the place for a busy Saturday market, where you can buy 'clootie dumpling like your Granny used to make' or 'finest quality whiting 5 lb only £7' which is certainly more than your Granny used to pay.

Perhaps the greatest building achievement of burgh times at Govan was the subway system, still widely used as a means of city transport, with Govan Cross one of the busiest stations. The system was designed and engineered by David Morton for the Glasgow and District Subway Company with twin circular tunnels $6^{1}/_{2}$ miles long and serving 15 stations. The first train left Govan Cross at 5 am on 14 December 1896 and 4,000 passengers used the trains in the first four hours. The subway was bought over by Glasgow Corporation in 1922, electrified in 1934, and extensively refurbished in the late 1970s. The subway workshops are still active on the original site in Broomloan Road, and the system is fully explained in a permanent exhibition in the Transport Museum. No trace now remains of Govan Railway Station or Goods Station, both built at Govan Cross for the Glasgow & Paisley Joint Railway around 1868, nor of the tramway which carried shipyard traffic along Govan Road to Fairfield's. A branch line crossed the road to Harland & Wolff's Yard and a small section of the track can still be seen crossing Water Row.

To the west of the Cross is the Pearce Institute, gifted to the people of Govan in 1906 by Lady Pearce and designed by Robert Rowand Anderson to resemble a large 17th-century town house. Inscribed on the entrance wall are the words:

> This is a House of Friendship. This is a House of Service.
> For Families. For Lonely Folk. For the people of Govan.
> For the Strangers of the World. Welcome.

The Institute still provides a welcome to the many individuals and community groups who use the restaurant, recreational facilities, the Lithgow Theatre, and the MacLeod Hall with its fine organ, stage and gallery. The Institute retains its traditional links with the Old Parish Church and the administrative head-quarters of the Iona Community are within the building.

Directly across the street is the statue of Sir William Pearce, erected in 1894 and locally known as the 'Black Man' due to the discoloration of the bronze. It stands on the corner of the Auld Causeway, renamed Morrison Street and later Burleigh Street after the Liberal opponent whom Pearce narrowly defeated in the 1885 parliamentary election. Behind is Brechin's Bar, on the site of Oakum Row. Above the Bar are the old Cardell Halls, originally built as a headquarters for temperance workers. Carved on the Burleigh Street side of the halls, and overhanging the eaves, is the famous Govan cat, a champion ratter with one of its victims in its mouth. Brechin's was famous, or infamous, as the first Govan pub to allow ladies on the premises, in a little alcove called the Snug. It has also been used as a set for films and TV productions.

Just along Govan Road is St Anthony's Catholic Parish Church, built at the corner of Harmony Row in 1879, from a design by John Honeyman. The church has an attractive bell tower and a rich interior, including a marble-lined apse and giant Corinthian columns in the nave. The presbytery and the school were added later.

The County Bingo building at the corner of McKechnie Street was formerly the Lyceum Cinema, built in 1938 and the last cinema in Govan to close in 1981. Its predecessor on the site was the Lyceum Music Hall, which opened in 1899 with a performance of *Carmen* given by the Carl Rosa Opera Company before an audience of 3,000 including Provost Kirkwood and the Govan Town Council. The Lyceum was also a venue for Irish plays such as *The Shaugraun* and *The Wearin' of the Green*. Three years later a 'biomotograph' was introduced which enabled Govanites to watch 'movies' such as a replay of a Scotland versus Wales football international and travel views. The three other Govan cinemas have all been demolished: the Elder in Rathlin Street, the Plaza at the Cross, and the Vogue at the corner of Langlands Road and Crossloan Road.

Abraham Hill was a successful merchant and native of Govan, who left money to purchase land, the rents from which paid for the education of ten poor children, by preference named Hill. After 1872 the Govan School Board used the Hill Trust money to build and endow a school in Golspie Street. Before 1872, the parish school was a two-storey building at Govan Cross, and the last parochial schoolmaster was William Fulton, a college-bred man and a bachelor, 'who solaced himself with a pipe after hours, and his preference was for black twist that had been moistened with Jamaica rum'. The Hill's Trust School is now in use as a Neighbourhood Centre and the name has been transferred to the modern primary school nearby.

Govan High School stood in Langlands Road from 1910 until 1962 when it was gutted by a fire which started in the science laboratory at the top of the building. A new health clinic has been built on the site and a replacement school erected in Ardnish Street, off Shieldhall Road. St Gerard's Catholic Secondary School in Vicarfield Street was built in 1937.

Linthouse and Shieldhall

Following the establishment of the shipyards on the west of Govan, the Linthouse and Shieldhall estates were developed for housing and industry. Linthouse was a small estate of around 20 acres, with rights to salmon fishing in the Clyde. The mansion house was designed for Mr Spreull by Robert Adam in 1791, and later became the residence of Michael Rowand, the cashier of the Ship Bank. This was the period when Linthouse became notorious for its 'Poison Pen' scandals, when the seeds of discord were widely sown throughout the whole community, resulting in numerous law-suits. The culprit was eventually identified as a Miss Hutton, a woman of 'spiteful, malignant temper' who resided in the house of a relative, 'worthy old George Rowan of Holmfauld–head' and was 'deep in all the clishmaclaver of the parish'. In 1868 the estate became the property of Stephen & Sons, who used the house as offices. After the company demolished the house, the portico was preserved and erected in Elder Park in 1921.

In 1872 Govan Poorhouse was built at Merryflats just to the south of Linthouse as a replacement for its predecessor which was housed in the old Cavalry Barracks at Gorbals. Merryflats served until 1930 as a poorhouse, hospital and asylum for the huge combined parishes of Govan and Gorbals. The original building still survives as part of the Southern General Hospital complex.

Two churches were built in Linthouse as the population grew. St Kenneth's was built in 1898 and became the parish church in

1915, and Linthouse Free Church was erected in 1899 for a congregation which had begun as a mission attached to St Mary's in
Govan. The two congregations united in 1976 and the St Kenneth's
building was demolished. The congregation of Linthouse St
Kenneth's now worship in the Linthouse church in Skipness Drive.
Shieldhall and Drumoyne United Free Church in Langcroft Road
was built in 1966 when an earlier church built in 1932 was
demolished for the road works in connection with the building of
the Clyde tunnel.

Linthouse, it is said, was known to Govanites as 'the Garden
of Eden'. The tenements were of red sandstone and had 'wally'
closes, and pre-war the area was 'dry'. The tunnel was responsible
for the demolition of some of these fine tenements, but despite
the loss, the community has kept its own identity, and the
Linthouse Community Trust organises events in Elder Park and
elsewhere.

Shieldhall was an older, early 18th-century house which came
into the ownership of the Oswald family. Around 1887 the estate
was purchased by the Scottish Wholesale Co-operative Society as
a site for a large industrial estate. The factory was a major employer
in the area, manufacturing a vast range of products for their stores:
furniture, clothes, tobacco products, and a range of food which
included coffee essence, pickles, confectionery and preserves.
Only two of the 30 or so red brick buildings remain.

Laughter and tears

In Govan, as elsewhere, much early entertainment took place in
the streets. Just beside the fountain at Govan Cross, Sequah, a
quack doctor, carried out the painless extraction of teeth. A loud
band played while he performed the operation. The visits of two
swarthy Basques from the Pyrenees with their dancing bears were
eagerly awaited by the crowds of children who followed them
through the streets. Outside the Sheephead Inn was the favourite
stage of Old Malabar, an Irish-born street entertainer, who stood
well over six feet tall and performed his acts dressed in colourful
Oriental costume. *HMS Malabar* was well known as an armed
troopship Napiers had built to carry soldiers to India. The Govan
Irish Club held their activities in a building entered through a pend
from Neptune Street, which because of its large immigrant
population was known as the 'Irish Channel'.

Amongst the earliest sports clubs in Govan were the Govan Bowling Club established in 1852, and the Bellahouston Bowling Club in 1858. The Bellahouston Harriers were formed in 1892 and the Govan police Tug-of-War team played annual fixtures with teams from Belfast and Dublin. The result depended on whether the visiting team got a smooth or a rough sea crossing. Rangers Football Club moved to their present stadium at Ibrox in 1899 and many of the large works and yards provided sports grounds for their employees. Govan's 'Old Firm' Benburb Juniors and St Anthony's Juniors, were founded in 1900 and 1902 respectively. The 'Bens' play at Tinto Park and the 'Ants' at Moore Park and compete annually with others for the 'Govan Fair Charity Cup'.

There have been times in Govan when real-life drama and tragedy have struck: twice on land, at Ibrox Stadium; twice at sea with the capsizing of the *Daphne* and the sinking of the K-13. The first Ibrox disaster happened during a Scotland versus England International in April 1902. At half-time a portion of the west terracing gave way without warning and 25 people were killed and many more injured. At that time the terracing was not made of earthworks but of wooden scaffolding and many of the spectators were thrown to the ground and crushed by the heavy beams. It was decided best to continue the match, which ended in a draw. Most of the crowd went home unaware of the accident and learned of the loss of life from the evening papers.

At the traditional game between Rangers and Celtic on New Year's Day 1971, disaster struck again, this time on Staircase Thirteen, the exit nearest to Copland Road subway. Of the 66 soccer fans who died, 32 were teenagers. The accident happened at the end of the match, when Rangers fans, hearing about their team's last-minute equaliser, ran back up the stairs into the path of thousands coming down. Somebody tripped and fell. The iron stanchions broke and disaster followed. Among the victims were a man and his young son, home on holiday from Canada to Govan for the first time since emigrating seven years before, and five teenage schoolboys all from the same street in Markinch in Fife, members of the Glenrothes branch of Rangers Supporters' Club. The only woman victim was an 18-year old girl from Maddiston, Falkirk. Ibrox Park is now a 51,000 all seater stadium. A memorial will be erected in 1996 to those who lost their lives on Staircase Thirteen in 1971.

The memorial to the men who lost their lives on the submarine K-13 during trials in the Gareloch in 1915. Six Fairfield's employees and 26 naval personnel are listed.

Accidents on the river were not uncommon in Govan. In 1861 seven of Napier's workmen were drowned transferring to the ferry from the steamer *Lochgoil*, which had brought them up from their work on the *Black Prince*, fitting out at Greenock. On Tuesday 3 July 1883, a much greater tragedy was to occur. Just after noon, the *Daphne*, a small steam coaster being built at Stephen's yard, heeled over after launching and rolled over completely in the river. Trapped aboard were nearly 200 workmen who were to have continued work on the ship as she was moved upriver to the Broomielaw for completion in time for the Glasgow Fair holiday. Despite frantic rescue efforts, a total of 124 men and boys lost their lives in the accident, one of the worst shipyard tragedies ever. The inquiry found that the cause was initial instability, coupled with an excess of persons and loose equipment aboard, Regulations covering launches were tightened. The ship was raised, repaired, renamed *Rose* and sold.

Inside the Elder Park, opposite Fairfield's offices, is a memorial to the men who lost their lives on the K-13, including six of the 14 employees of the company who were on board. The K-13 was a submarine, one of two vessels of the double-hull type ordered by the Admiralty from the Fairfield Company late in 1915. She was notable both for her size and for her method of propulsion, being over 330 feet in length, of 2,600 tons displacement, driven on the surface by steam turbines and when submerged by storage batteries and electric motors.

On 29 January 1916, during trials in the Gareloch, the boiler room flooded and K-13 sank out of control in nearly 60 feet of water. On board were 80 naval personnel and civilians. The 48 survivors were kept alive during their 55 hour ordeal by the technical knowledge, skill and ingenuity of Percy Hillhouse, Fairfield's Naval Architect, and the other Fairfield men, 'who knew every pipe, and valve and switch in the vessel' and kept going the air supply and the electric light. The memorial has the names of the men lost, including the Captain of the K-14, Commander Goodhart, who was on board the K-13 as an observer, and who was postumously awarded the Albert Medal for his gallantry in an unsuccessful attempt to reach the surface by way of the conning tower.

The Govan Weavers and the Govan Fair

The Govan Weavers' Society and the Govan Fair have both played an important part in the history of the village. The Weavers' Society was formed in 1756 with the dual purpose of regulating entry into the trade and providing for weavers fallen on hard times. The first collector was Robert Rowand and the funds came from quarterly payments and the proceeds of the swear box. The society is still in existence, and among the items collected over the years is the famous Sheep's Head, the emblem of the Society. The tale goes that when the minister refused a young woman in his service permission to marry, the people of the village sided with the young couple, and in retaliation cut off the head of every sheep in the

St Gerard's School's prize-winning float in the Govan Fair procession in June 1995.

minister's glebe. The choicest sheep's head was selected to be paraded by posterity, on top of a pole at the front of each succeeding Govan Fair Day procession. At the traditional meal consumed by the weavers at their annual meeting on Fair Night, one of the delicacies was boiled eggs washed down with 'White Wine'.

The origins of the Govan Fair are lost in the mists of time, but the fair may have been granted by some church authority at the end of the 15th century. The Fair was revived by the weavers on the first Friday of June 1757. It lapsed in 1881, but was revived again in 1921 and since 1968 has been carried on by the Govan Fair Association, with the proceeds going to charity. Nowadays one of the highlights is the crowning of the Govan Fair Queen. The Queen in 1995 was Sheryl Dickie with attendants from Elder Park School, and she was crowned on Friday 2 June by Teri Lally, star of the popular television series *Take the High Road*. Previous celebrities who have crowned the Queen include footballers Alex Ferguson and David Hay.

After the crowning ceremony in the Victory Christian Centre, the procession travelled the length of Govan Road on the two and a half mile route to the saluting base in Copland Road. Winners of

A smart group of majorettes stepping out on Govan Fair Day in June 1995.

the best floats were St Gerard's School, Scottish Pride Netball Team, and the California Cake & Cookie Company, and in the music sections, Kinning Park Pipe Band, Prince of Wales Accordion Band, and the 1990 Glasgow Steel Band. Winner of the majorettes event was the Michelle McNeill School of Dance, followed by the Avril McGeorge School of Dance and the Bridgeton Majorettes. The nursery prize was won by Broomloan Road Nursery. Benburb defeated St Anthony's in the Charity Football, Sandwood School won the netball, first in the Ladies' Bowling was Bellahouston with Fairfield runners-up and Govan won the Gents Bowling. The Govan Fair Association also runs the largest netball tournament in Britain with heats run over three nights and the final usually on the Sunday after the Fair. An impressive record for a lively and justifiably proud community with roots stretching far into the past.

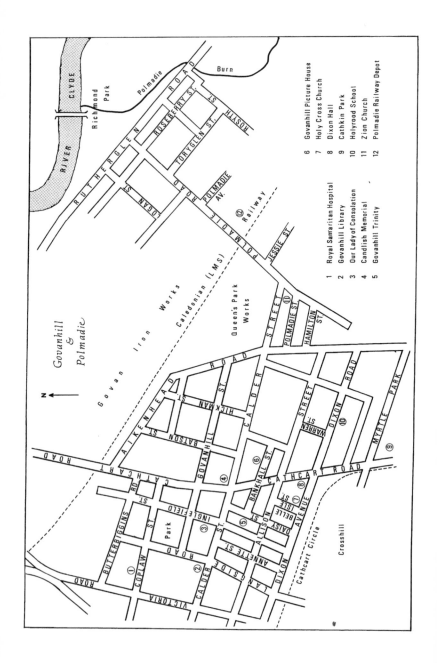

Govanhill & Polmadie

1 Royal Samaritan Hospital
2 Govanhill Library
3 Our Lady of Consolation
4 Candlish Memorial
5 Govanhill Trinity
6 Govanhill Picture House
7 Holy Cross Church
8 Dixon Hall
9 Cathkin Park
10 Holyrood School
11 Zion Church
12 Polmadie Railway Depot

CHAPTER 5

GOVANHILL AND POLMADIE

Govanhill began as a small colliers' village built by William Dixon, a native of Tyneside, for his workers in the Little Govan Colliery which he managed from the early 1770s and of which he was the sole owner from 1820. The little village was known locally as the Fireworks. It consisted of several miners' rows set astride the Cathcart Road between what are now Allison Street and Calder Street. The rows on the east side of Cathcart Road were placed round the Colliery Yard which also contained the head offices of the company, workshops, the manager's house, and a larger house called Bankhall. The present Bankhall Street runs through the centre of the site. These rows were named the Engine Row, the Carter Row, the Cuddy Row, the Back Close and Graham Square. The rows on the west side of Cathcart Road were named Hosie's Land and Garden Square. A little further north, still on the west side of the main road, between what is now Calder Street and Govanhill Street, were more miners' houses at School Square, with the Colliers' School just immediately to the north.

William Dixon bought the Govanhill estate along with the colliery around 1820. He already owned several other collieries and the Calder Iron Works in Lanarkshire, and at his death in 1824 was considered the largest coal and iron master in the west of Scotland. About half the coal was exported to towns along the Clyde and Ireland. Because the Broomielaw was too shallow for shipping his coals, Dixon constructed a horse-drawn waggonway from the Little Govan Colliery via West Street to the river at Windmillquay. In the 1830s William Dixon's son, also William, who continued and expanded the business, upgraded and extended his father's waggonway to form the Pollok and Govan railway. This later formed part of the main Caledonian line from the south into Glasgow Central. In 1839 Dixon started the Govan Iron Works about half a mile north of Fireworks village. The glare in the sky at night from the five blast furnaces was for long a famous Glasgow landmark. Much of the ironstone was mined nearby 'in the ground running towards Polmadie' and both pig-iron and malleable iron was produced. Dixon appears to have brought many men from the Shropshire area of England to carry out the new techniques of puddling the crude iron to produce the more valuable malleable iron for use in the forge. William Mann, the manager of the Iron Works was a Glasgow man, and occupied Inglefield House to the north of Butterbiggins Road. Inglefield Street was laid out for tenement building in the 1870s, but the house survived into the 1930s.

According to the census taken in 1841, 134 families, about 600 people, lived at the Fireworks. About 160 of the men were coal miners, and of the other 35 working men, twelve were engine keepers and other-trades included a hammerman, an engineer, a weigher on the railway, a smith and a joiner. Two-thirds of the villagers had been born in the parish, and only 46 persons were of Irish birth.

When Thomas Tancred, HM Inspector of Mines, visited Govan Colliery in 1842, there were 808 employees, living at Fireworks and other mining villages in the area, of whom 49 were below 13 years of age. Most boys began work about nine years, and no females were employed. Tancred spoke to Robert Ferguson, who told him that he came down the pit at three in the morning and sometimes worked as late as six in the evening. Ferguson and his brother worked together and had four drawers to pull the loaded waggons to the shaft. Three were his younger brothers aged 17, 15 and 12, but the fourth was a boy of 11, whose father was in the iron-works, and not related. The boy lived with Ferguson, was clothed and fed, but not paid any wages. Ferguson explained that he 'just has the boy for his meat, and may keep him all his days if he likes it'.

Tancred also spoke to Francis Connery, aged nine, who was a trapper, and whose task was to open and shut the trap-door again when the whirleys went past. Francis was in the pit from 6 am to 6 pm.

> He sits on a board in a niche in the wall without a light, quite in the dark, and holds a rope, and so opens the door, and when the carriage has passed he shuts it again. He has some bread, tea, and cheese, sent down by the engine and brought to him by a drawer, or if slack he can run and get it himself. It serves him for the day, as long as he is down the pit.

Dixon required all colliers and others employed at the Govan

The five blast furnaces of Dixon's Iron Works, which were begun on a 'green-field' site in 1839. These were the last Glasgow iron-works to close in 1958. From William Simpson's Glasgow in the Forties.

Colliery to adhere to a set of printed rules. The collier had to give 14 days notice before he could leave his employment, and was given 14 days intimation to leave the colliery and remove from his house and garden. No connection was allowed with any society which might interfere with the employer's right to employ or discharge his workmen. Employees had to contribute to a Friendly Society and a Funeral Fund, and pay school fees for each child from six to twelve years of age. But attendance at day school was reported as irregular. On average only half the children attended. Night school was poorly attended.

The miners normally worked ten days in twelve. For their leisure hours Mr Dixon provided a library managed by the men themselves, where they could read two daily London papers, the *Times* and the *Morning Chronicle*, and several periodicals, such as *John Bull*. There was also a band of about 25 instruments and a violin band of six or seven besides a bass. Every other Saturday the schoolmaster and the clerk at the forge gave a lecture on scientific subjects, illustrated by magic lantern. A season ticket cost one shilling and the evening's entertainment was rounded off with recitation, sentimental and comic singing and other amusements.

By the late 1860s the coal was worked out and William Smith Dixon, grandson of the founder, feued out the Govanhill estate for tenement housing. This led to the disappearance of the old rows. Garden Square disappeared about 1880 and the blocks at School Square ten years later. Hosie's Land behind the Dixon Hall was razed in 1907 and Graham Square was the last to go in 1909. Several new streets were named after persons and places connected with the Dixon family: Calder Street after Dixon's Lanarkshire estate; Belleisle Street after the estate of William Smith Dixon near Ayr; Annette Street and Daisy Street after his daughters; Hickman Street and Morgan Street after a member of the family, Mrs Hickman Morgan. Allison Street is thought to be associated with Sir Archibald Allison, Sheriff-Principal of Lanarkshire. The Govanhill tenements were generally of superior construction. Houses were required to have at least two rooms and all were to have internal sanitation. Govanhill remains the best preserved area of working class tenements in the city.

The Govan Iron Works were taken over by Colvilles and were the last blast furnace to operate within the Glasgow city boundary. The works closed in 1958 and 'Dixon's Blazes' with their distinctive smoke and 'fitful clouds of sparks' thrown up into the night sky made way for the Castle Cash & Carry.

Govanhill Burgh: Fireworks to No Man's Land

Fireworks was the name given to Govanhill until the 1860s. The area then became known as No Man's Land. This name came about when neighbouring Crosshill, in Renfrewshire, became a burgh in 1871. Govanhill, in Lanarkshire, was not populous enough to be granted burgh status, and became isolated between the City of Glasgow and the Burgh of Crosshill, neglected and with no powers to run its own affairs. In the 1870s there are frequent complaints about the condition of the roads, lack of lighting and cleansing, and hints about houses of ill-fame which the police, under the County Police Act, were powerless to deal with.

With the boom in tenement building in the 1870s, however, Govanhill grew in size and was able to achieve burgh status on 4 July 1877. A police office was speedily erected off Belleisle Street, with cells for prisoners and a tenement of houses for the constables. Premises were also acquired for a fire brigade and a scavenging department. James Smith Dixon gifted a site at the junction of Dixon Avenue and Cathcart Road for a Burgh Hall to be shared between the Burghs of Govanhill and Crosshill. The building was to be erected in such a way that half was in the county of Lanark and half in the county of Renfrew. Each burgh would have its own entrance and its offices in its own county. The Dixon Hall was opened in December 1879 at a ceremony attended by Provost and Mrs Browne of Govanhill, Provost and Mrs Smith of Crosshill, and other dignitaries, but unfortunately Mr Dixon was prevented by illness from being present. Two years later Govanhill Burgh was extended eastwards as far as the Little Govan Burn (Jenny's Burn) on the boundary with Rutherglen, despite an objection by Messrs Dubs & Co, whose Queen's Park Locomotive Works at Polmadie then occupied much of the area added. Govanhill was itself annexed, along with Crosshill, to Glasgow in 1891. This ended the complaints of the citizens of Glasgow about being 'cabined, cribbed, and confined' by a circle of upstart burghs, sharing its wealth, and more than a fair share of its privileges, without paying a farthing in return.

Newspapers of the 1880s report the usual problems of burgh management: there should be a public library to keep the noisy youth better employed by night and on Saturday afternoons; there should be one or two fountains for pure water, as in hot weather a drink of water has to be paid for in shops 'where they dare not drink it' and it might also save dram-drinking up closes and 'the bottle-smashing business, which the district is alone famous for'; Cathcart Road south of Allison Street is too narrow, cars and carts eternally pass, and boisterous mobs pass on Saturdays to football matches. Another persistent complaint concerns the want of a public clock. 'Glasgow has scores, Pollokshields has a few, every little town has one, even the queer folk in the 'Shaws are not without it'. Provost Hunter suggested a clock tower on the tenement being built at the corner of Bankhall Street and Cathcart Road; Bailie Murray suggested the Candlish Memorial Free Church spire, but Commissioner McNaughton thought the Established Church a more suitable spot; Bailie Whyte, supported by Bailie Copestake, thought the Burgh Hall Tower the proper place; and Commissioner Duncan moved that a committee be formed to look out for a suitable location.

Much social life centred on the Dixon Hall, where either burgh could have the use of the central hall. This was the venue for the

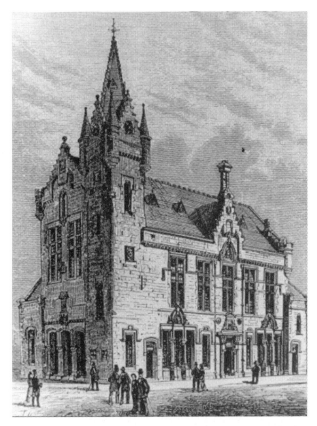

The Dixon Hall was gifted by W S Dixon and built exactly on the boundary between Govanhill and Crosshill to serve both burghs. Each burgh had its own entrance and offices. Now a day centre for the elderly.

annual Conversazione of the Govanhill West Ward. A lady and gentleman's ticket cost 7s 6d, a lady's ticket 2s 6d. Tea was served at 7.30, dancing began at 8 o'clock, and carriages at 2.30 am. The menu for a complimentary dinner for Mr Walter Haxton was as follows:

fish course - dressed cod and oyster sauce or filleted soles
entree - mutton cutlets and tomatoes or curried chicken
joint - roast beef, corned beef, turkey and tongue or roast chicken
sweet - plum pudding, hot apple souffle, Swiss tart, German tart, jellies or creams
fruit to follow.

Another highlight was the annual Children's Ball, given for his small pupils by Mr R M Sellars. This took place not in the Dixon Hall, but in the 3rd LRV drill hall, and was attended in 1889 by 200 children who began queuing outside from half past three. The Ball began at five o'clock with the Grand March. The spectators' sitting and standing room was filled to see little maidens in dainty frocks, magnificent sashes, silk stockings and tiny slippers, and small boys in kilts, Eton suits and white waistcoats. Some of the children were only four years of age and it was a 'caution' to see them waltzing and dancing the gavotte, and the boys taking each his partner's hand with all the gallantry of a 17th-century courtier. Their mamas and papas wept with pride. The Ball was an immense success and broke up about 10 o'clock.

The complaints about boisterous football fans passing down Cathcart Road on Saturdays were no doubt directed towards the Spiders, supporters of Queen's Park, or the Hi-Hi's, supporters of Third Lanark. Queen's Park, Scotland's first football club, formed in 1867, played in black and white. The Third Lanark Football Club began in 1872 as the regimental team of the Third Lanarkshire Rifle Volunteers, and adopted a uniform of the regimental colours, 'scarlet jersey and blue knickerbockers'. This later became a red jersey and white shorts. The team played on a pitch at the west end of the drill ground, which was a former brickfield in the area between Allison Street and Dixon Road. Third Lanark was the fifth club to be formed in Scotland, was a founder member of the SFA, and won the Scottish Cup in 1889, defeating Celtic 2-1 in the final. In 1903 the club crossed over the boundary into Crosshill to take over the football ground at Cathkin when Queen's Park moved to a new stadium at Hampden. Third Lanark then celebrated by winning the League in 1903–04 and the Cup again in 1905 with a 3-1 win over Rangers.

Third Lanark were relegated to the Second Division in 1965, and disbanded two years later. Cathkin Park now contains a modern recreation centre and is used for a variety of recreational and educational purposes. Outside the entrance to the park is a paved area into which is set, in metal studs, the badge of the Third Lanarkshire Rifle Volunteers, with the number 3 in the centre and a crown above. Within the park the famous pitch is still in use by Junior teams. Parts of the terracing remain intact on three sides, complete with iron rails to lean on and nostalgically recall former glories.

Churches and Schools

In striking contrast to its neighbour the Gorbals, Govanhill has succeeded in preserving most of its Victorian church buildings, although many have now been converted to other use, mainly as premises for social services. Regrettably the earliest church in Govanhill has been destroyed. This was the Wesleyan Methodist Church at the south-west corner of Cathcart Road and Butterbiggins Road, which first appears on Glasgow post office maps in 1863, and may have included amongst its members the English workers at the Govan Iron Works. George Whitefield, the celebrated Wesleyan preacher and evangelist, is supposed to have occupied Crosshill House, later owned by the Dixons, during his several visits to the Glasgow district in the 1740s.

In the remarkable period of expansion of Govanhill in the 1870s, the Free Church, the Established Church and the United Presbyterian Church each formed a congregation within the space of two years and built its own church within about two hundred yards of each other. After a series of mergers, their successors now worship together as one congregation in Govanhill Trinity Church in the former UP building in Daisy Street under the ministry of the Rev Thomas Bisek. The Daisy Street church was built in 1880 to a design by Robert Baldie and has a handsome interior with the seating following a horseshoe plan. It also contains the 1914–18 War Memorial which was moved from the former Parish Church when the two congregations were united in 1952. The Parish Church, which was opened in 1881 at the corner of Allison Street and Cathcart Road, was later demolished and Govanhill Nursery School built on the site. The Candlish Memorial Church was named in memory of a leading Free Church minister and opened in 1877 The design was by John Honeyman and the handsome spire still forms a landmark at the corner of Calder Street and Cathcart Road. The church has lain empty since the recent merger of the congregation as part of Govanhill Trinity, and its future is uncertain. Candlish Memorial formed a previous union with Eglinton-Elgin Church of Scotland in 1953 and with Polmadie Church of Scotland in 1968. Polmadie was begun as yet another United Presbyterian mission which met in a small hall from 1883. A church was built in Calder Street near Polmadie Road in 1897. After the union with Candlish Memorial, the Polmadie buildings were sold and are now occupied by the Sovereign Grace Baptist Zion Church under the ministry of Pastor Jack Glass.

Govanhill Free Church of Scotland in Belleisle Street has its name carved on the wall in distinctive 'Glasgow Style' lettering with the date 1909. The United Free Church at 62 Daisy Street was formed by a union of the members of the Candlish Memorial and the New Bridgegate United Free Church congregations who remained outside the union with the Established Church in 1929. The origins of the New Bridgegate church are in the Free Wynd congregation whose roots go back as far as 1685 in the area south of the Trongate. After their church was acquired by a railway company, the New Bridgegate congregation moved in 1921 to Govanhill and built a church in Dixon Road at Warren Street. This church is now closed and has become Govanhill Workspace, used by a firm of architects. Incorporated in the outside wall of the church is the stone bookrest from the outdoor stone pulpit from which the minister of the original church in the Bridgegate used to deliver his open air sermons to his flock.

Among the other churches converted to new uses are the former Forsyth Memorial Congregational Church at 149 Coplaw Street, which is now the offices of the Govanhill Housing Association. The memorial stone laid on 5 September 1903 by Mrs Hickman Morgan has been retained on the facade. St Martin's Episcopal Church on Dixon Road at Aikenhead Road has been converted to housing. The former Baptist Church built on Butterbiggins Road at Langside Road in 1897 became a Masonic Hall and is now the Central Mosque Khazra, and the former Church of Christ at 70 Coplaw Street serves as the Namdev Cultural Centre.

The first Catholic church in Govanhill was Holy Cross chapel and school in Daisy Street just north of Govanhill Trinity Church. An additional school building was added in 1900 at the corner of Calder Street. These buildings are now used for social work. To meet the needs of the expanding Catholic population of the district, a new Holy Cross Church was erected in 1911 to a design by Pugin & Pugin. In completely contrasting style, Our Lady of Consolation Church was built in 1971 in Inglefield Street, with the church at first floor level, reached from a car park at ground level. The church is built on the site of the old Majestic Picture House.

Three of the four buildings erected by the Govan Parish School Board in Govanhill following the Education Act of 1872, remain

A view from the top of Govanhill Street over the new houses between Batson Street and Cathcart Road. The view includes the spire of the Candlish Memorial Church.

in use as schools. The exception is the original Calder Street Public School building erected in 1874, which is now used for social work. This is the twin-gabled building with distinctive spiral chimneys adjacent to the Candlish Memorial Church. The school was replaced in 1914 by a new red-sandstone school on the south side of Calder Street also bearing the name Calder Street Public School, but locally known as Batson Street School. This is now Holy Cross Primary School. Govanhill Public School, now Annette Street Primary, was built in 1886 and was intended for use by the children of both Govanhill and Crosshill. This imposing three storey school was designed by H & D Barclay. Victoria Public School, now Victoria Primary, is also a red sandstone building, erected in 1903 at the top of Govanhill Street in the area then known as Victoria Gardens. Holybrooke School is a special school housed in a modern building nearby and Holyrood Secondary School was built in Dixon Road in 1936.

Govanhill has retained intact not only its tenements, but also many of its public buildings. The Calder Street baths are still in use, although the 'Steamie' behind is now a launderette. Another well-known building, the Royal Samaritan Hospital for Women,

Customers and shop assistants outside 'The Fruit Market' in Allison Street. This is one of the best preserved streets of working-class tenement housing in the city.

awaits development as flats or as a hotel. The hospital was originally built in Hutchesontown for the care of poor women of the district and transferred to its new home in Butterbiggins Road in 1896. The Nurses Homes on the corner of Victoria Road were the gift of Mrs Cameron Corbett of Rowallan and their round towers reflect the style of Rowallan House. The handsome Govanhill Library on the corner of Calder Street and Langside Road, the work of James Rhind, caters today for the expanding Asian community by maintaining a large collection of Urdu, Punjabi, Hindu and Chinese material, along with spoken word and music tapes and daily newspapers in Urdu and Chinese and a selection of periodicals. Many of the Hindus, Sikhs and Moslems who came to settle in Glasgow after the partition of India in 1947 and the passing of the British Nationality Act in 1948, found employment on public transport, working at the large Larkfield bus depot and living in the Gorbals before moving out to Govanhill. The most commonly spoken language among Asians in Glasgow is Punjabi. Urdu and Punjabi and some other Asian languages are taught in several secondary schools in the city and there are bi-lingual teachers in some primary schools.

View west along Bankhall Street to Govanhill Trinity Church. This area was formerly the yard of the Little Govan Colliery and contained several miners' rows.

Govanhill largely escaped the comprehensive development policy favoured by Glasgow Corporation up to the 1970s, although some tenement areas on the east side of Cathcart Road were lost. The building of new houses on this sloping site continues immediately north of Calder Street. Govanhill Housing Association was formed in 1974 to oversee the refurbishment of the tenement stock. Near Govanhill Park modern tenements have been skilfully integrated with the older buildings such as in Annandale Street where modern buildings enclose a Victorian tenement. In the park itself refurbishment is underway to use the four acres to provide a seating area, all weather pitches and a toddlers' play area. After consultation with the local community, a similar park was designed by the Parks and Recreation Department of the City Council and opened in 1994 at Riccarton Street.

As elsewhere in the city, most of the Govanhill picture houses have gone. The BB Cinerama, for example, at Eglinton Toll, was a 2,700 seat cinema which opened in 1912 and was one of Glasgow's longest running cinemas until closure in 1981. BB stood for 'Bright and Beautiful' and the cinema had a rising sun decoration above the original entrance in Butterbiggins Road. One surviving cinema is the former Govanhill Picture House in Bankhall Street. The white painted oriental-style building with its tiled Egyptian frontage and

Hindu-inspired domes, was an ABC cinema opened in 1926 to seat 1,200. It closed in 1981 and is now used as a warehouse for Goldtext Fabrics. Another cinema, the Calder, was built back to back with the Govanhill, but is now demolished. Also gone are the Majestic or 'Magic Stick' in Inglefield Street and the Hampden in Westmorland Street.

Bankhall Street sums up the story of Govanhill: fine red sandstone tenements in the best Glasgow style, with 'wally' closes, decorative medallions between the second and third floor stonework and ornamental ironwork just below roof level; a Govan Board school; an exotic 1920s cinema; and at the end of the street Govanhill Trinity Church and the Holy Cross chapel school. All this where once stood the colliers' rows in the little miners' village that once was 'Fireworks'.

'Out o' the world and into Polmadie'

The name of Polmadie is mentioned as one of the boundaries of the territory which David I gave to his burgesses in Rutherglen when he gave the Royal Burgh its charter in 1126. The Polmadie Burn which formed the ancient boundary was also known as Mall's Myre Burn and is still referred to as Jenny's Burn, although Jenny's identity remains a secret. From its origins near Aikenhead the burn runs through Mount Florida and joins the river Clyde just west of the Polmadie Bridge, a foot-bridge which crosses the river between Glasgow Green and Richmond Park. It is now culverted for much of its course, but is still visible passing through Richmond Park.

When Robert I visited Rutherglen in 1316, he confirmed a charter of Alexander III which showed that a hospital dedicated to St John existed at Polmadie as early as 1249. This was a place of refuge for poor men and women, and possibly also a place of accommodation for pilgrims and travellers. The charter also confirms the rights of the hospital to the 'goods belonging to them in Strablathy (Strathblane) or any other place'. Four years later King Robert's friend and staunch supporter, Bishop John Wishart of Glasgow, further endowed the hospital with the 'eastern part of the lands of Little Govan'. This was roughly the ground covered by modern Polmadie, and shortly after, the hospital also received the lands of Corshill (Crosshill). Patrick Floker was appointed guardian of the house 'with the power of restraining the excesses and correcting the faults of the brethern and sister pensioners

113

therein, or of removing any of them for their delinquency'.

About 1450 the endowments and lands of the Polmadie hospital were transferred to a new Collegiate Church at Dumbarton. It is possible that Glasgow now cared for its poor and aged at St Nicholas hospital, which was founded about this time beside Glasgow Cathedral by Bishop Muirhead.

The exact location of Polmadie hospital is unknown, but it is likely to have been situated near the ancient highway which led along the south bank of the river Clyde from 'the monastery at Govane to the King's residence at Ruglan' and probably lay at the extremity of the Bishop's barony immediately west of the Polmadie Burn, the boundary with Rutherglen, hence the old saying, 'Out of the world and into Polmadie'.

The Polmadie Martyrs: Robert Thome, Thomas Cooke, John Urie

After the Reformation the lands of Polmadie and Crosshill were feued to Sir John Stewart of Minto and on Blaeu's map, surveyed by Pont in 1590, a house is shown at 'Pomadi'. According to a sketch map reproduced by A M Scott in his *Notes on the lands of Polmadie and Crosshill* in 1889, there was, by the end of the 17th century, a village of Polmadie near the west bank of the Polmadie Burn, about 300 yards south of Rutherglen Road. This is now the area between Toryglen Street and Rosyth Street. The plan also shows Polmadie Loan. The Loan ran west from the village to join the Aikenhead Road, and is today represented by a short remaining stretch of Polmadie Avenue. The purpose of the map is to illustrate an article in which Scott describes the events of 11 May 1685, when on the orders of Major John Balfour and Captain James Maitland, soldiers seized two weavers, Thomas Cooke and John Urie, in Polmadie village and caught Robert Thome, a land labourer, after a chase through the village. The men were taken along the loan and questioned on their Covenanting beliefs and alleged activities. They were then shot and their bodies taken to Cathcart kirkyard for burial. The stone over the Martyrs' Tomb tells the story:

> As soon as they had them out found
> They murthered them with shots of guns
> Scarce time did they to them allow
> Before ther maker ther knies to bow.

The deed was witnessed by two men at Polmadie Mill. The

mill stood on the right bank of the Polmadie Burn on the north side of Rutherglen Road, on the Shawfield estate. Millcroft Road perpetuates the name of the croft adjoining the mill.

Miners, railwaymen and engineers

On Richardson's map of 1795 the owner of the 'Polmadee' estate is shown as R H Rae, and shortly after, the property was acquired by Moses Steven of Bellahouston. In the 1850s the house was occupied by a tea merchant, Colin McLaws, and the last occupant at the end of the century appears to have been Alexander Fullarton, minister of the Buchanan Memorial Free Church. For much of the century the 120 acre Polmadie farm was farmed by the Jackson family.

When William Dixon began to work the Little Govan coalfield, part of his workforce were settled in a small colliers' village at Polmadie, convenient for working the pits at the east end of the colliery. In 1851 there were about 50 miners' families in Polmadie and two-thirds were Irish. The village was in two halves. The Scots miners and some of the Irish lived in two rows called Young's Row and Patterson's Row, built along the west side of Aikenhead Road approximately between the present Govanhill Street and Calder Street. The Scots were local men or had come from Monklands, Midlothian, Bo'ness, Polmont, Muirkirk and Dumfries. Most of the Irish families lived on the east side of Aikenhead Road in the area which was later built over by the Queen's Park Locomotive Works.

In 1848 the Caledonian Railway Company used part of Dixon's Pollok and Govan line to form their main line from Carlisle to Glasgow. In 1864 Henry Dubs, a German engineer who had been a partner in Walter Neilson's Hydepark Locomotive Works, set up the Queen's Park Locomotive Work just south of the Caledonian line and Polmadie soon became a major rival to Springburn. Dubs is remembered as one of the first to employ women in industry, training them to work as tracers in his drawing office. When he died in 1876, around one hundred locomotives a year were being built at Polmadie and the miners' village had become a railway town.

We're Railwaymen at Polmadie
In a hotter place you couldn'a be
And when in Hell we gather when we dee
We'll be nane the waur than in Polmadie

The 'Lady Dickson', a tank engine built by Dubs & Co in 1890 for the Sungei Ujong Railway in the Straits Settlements. Gauge 3ft, 3³/₈ins. Note the diamond-shaped nameplate of Dubs & Co at the rear of the cab.

After 1876 the firm was managed by William Lorimer, who had joined Dubs as an engineer in 1864 at the age of 20 years. Under Lorimer the business continued to produce locomotives for a world wide market, the exception being North America. By 1903 the company had around 2,500 employees on a 24 acre site. In the same year Dubs & Co amalgamated with two other companies, the Atlas Works and the Hyde Park Works, both at Springburn, to form the North British Locomotive Works, the largest locomotive engineering company in Europe, with Lorimer as chairman. As their name-plate the new company used the diamond shaped emblem which Dubs had adapted from the mark on the locally made bricks he used to build his first offices and works at Polmadie. Too much reliance on overseas markets and the failure to make the change to diesel and electric early enough weakened the firm and led to the closure of all three works in 1962.

Polmadie was a railway village which also built ships. At their Sentinel Works in Jessie Street, Messrs Alley & MacLellan operated 'a land-locked shipbuilding yard from which never a ship is launched, but where many a ship is built'. The yard built ships in sections, and pre-fabricated Polmadie-built vessels finished up being assembled on Lake Nyassa, Lake Baikal, and on the rivers of Brazil, Mexico, South Africa and Australia. The works were moved to Polmadie from Bridgeton around 1880 by Stephen Alley, an Irishman from County Kildare, who had learned his trade with A & J Inglis at Pointhouse and had also been a manager at Neilson's Hydepark Works. The firm was mainly an engineering works, with products such as high speed engines, hoists and excavators, and at one time employed nearly 900 men.

The Caledonian Railway was also a large employer in the area after it opened the Polmadie engine shed in 1879, incorporating a large repair shop. The site is now the Intercity Polmadie Depot where Railtrack make up the trains for Intercity. Other firms at present in Polmadie are the British Oxygen Company, the Cleansing Department Polmadie Depot, Mackay & Inglis Printers, and Hussman, who make commercial refrigeration equipment.

To house the growing population, streets of tenements were built at the north end of Polmadie Road in the 1890s. As part of the recent regeneration of the area, the tenements in Cramond Street were demolished and the vacant space between Rosebery Street and Toryglen Street grassed over. At the south end of Polmadie Road little is left of the original community. One solitary empty tenement remains in Hamilton Street containing Polmadie post office. A fire station has replaced the school in Polmadie Street and the only remaining church in use is the Sovereign Grace Baptist Zion Church which was built in 1895 as Polmadie United Presbyterian Church. St Margaret's Church in Polmadie Road is a B-listed building designed in 1902 by McGregor Chalmers. The church remains although the congregation was dissolved in 1984.

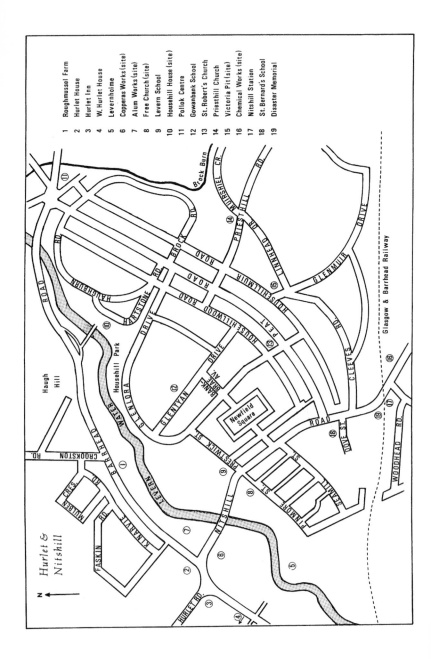

Hurlet & Nitshill

N

1	Roughmussel Farm
2	Hurlet House
3	Hurlet Inn
4	W. Hurlet House
5	Levernholme
6	Copperas Works (site)
7	Alum Works (site)
8	Free Church (site)
9	Levern School
10	Househill House (site)
11	Pollok Centre
12	Gowanbank School
13	St. Robert's Church
14	Priesthill Church
15	Victoria Pit (site)
16	Chemical Works (site)
17	Nitshill Station
18	St. Bernard's School
19	Disaster Memorial

CHAPTER 6
HURLET AND NITSHILL

The Hurlet and the Nitshill, as these two neighbouring villages are locally known, are situated just within the Glasgow city boundary, about two miles north of the town of Barrhead. Both were originally in the Abbey parish of Paisley, and were incorporated into Glasgow in 1926. Both villages began as small mining communities situated on the turnpike road from Paisley to East Kilbride, now the A726, near where the road crosses the Levern Water, a tributary of the White Cart. Hurlet, on the left bank of the river, grew up on the Hawkhead estate of the earls of Glasgow; Nitshill, on the right bank, less than a mile to the south-east, was situated on the Househill estate of the Dunlop family.

The villages developed rapidly as a result of early 19th century industrial development, supplying coal and building stone by canal and railway to the rapidly growing city of Glasgow. Still more significant was the establishment of large scale alum and copperas works along the banks of the Levern, producing the mordants used in the dyeing process by the numerous printfields in the vicinity and bringing in their train the inevitable industrial blight. Hugh MacDonald, travelling from Glasgow to Barrhead by railway in 1851, to begin one of his *Rambles*, describes the scene as

> the engine whirls us past the red hills of the Hurlet, amid sights and scents unholy, past Nitshill, with its quarries, coal-pits, and belching volumes of smoke, and about half-an-hour after starting, deposits us safely at Grahamstone, a clean and tidy-looking suburb of Barrhead, nestling finely at the base of the Fereneze Braes, and overlooking a picturesque sweep of the murmuring Levern.

In September 1858 quite a different group of excursionists visited the Hurlet. These were the gentlemen of the Geological Society of Glasgow, come to study glacial action. Fired with enthusiasm, the gentlemen returned the following week to visit the alum works. After arriving by train at Kennishead, and inspecting a quarry or two, the party walked to Hurlet, where the more active went down the Townhead pit on the alum shale. 'This was no joke, as the descent and ascent were made by a series of

Hurlet village stood at the junction of the road from Paisley to East Kilbride with the road from Barrhead to Glasgow. The new Hurlet Inn occupies the south-west corner of the crossroads.

ladders'. Two members unfortunately became separated from the main body, and the luckless pair were left in darkness and afraid to move until a search party was formed and, retracing their steps, 'the benighted men of science were soon relieved'.

The miners rows which formed Hurlet village have now given way to streets of 20th-century housing built over fields which were once part of Roughmussel farm. The site of the alum works was landscaped in the late 1960s to form a walkway along the ever-murmuring Levern. The coal-mining village that was 'Old Nitshill' has completely disappeared and the large sandstone quarry just to the south is now also a landscaped area in the vicinity of Cleeves Road. The centre of what was known as 'New Nitshill' is the area round Nitshill railway station and the nearby shops which today serve the large surrounding communities of 1930s and 1950s local authority housing. Remaining industry is located at the Darnley Industrial Estate and at South Nitshill Industrial Estate.

The coal miners: as heavy a darg as any in Scotland.

The Hawkhead or Hurlet coal seam extended over about 500 acres of land on the Hawkhead, Househill and Nether Pollok estates. In 1812 it was stated that coal had been wrought at Hawkhead for at least 300 years and a lease dated 1634 said that five miners were employed. In 1782 there were 24 families at the Hurlet, 'mostly employed in the great coal and lime work carried on by the Countess of Glasgow on her Hawkhead estate'. In 1793 a mine is mentioned at 'Nutshiel' belonging to James Dunlop of Househill, extending over 50 acres. New collieries were opened up on the Nether Pollok estate in the 19th century, wrought by Messrs John Wilson & Sons, who held them in lease from Sir John Maxwell.

In 1842 the Hurlet colliery operated by Messrs John Wilson & Sons was inspected as part of an official government inquiry into the employment of children in mines. At the Haugh pit, Peter Boag, bottom-man of the pit, explained to the Commissioner, Thomas Tancred, that the colliers' 'darg' or day's work, was 16 baskets per day, about as heavy as any in Scotland. The miners were paid from 3s 3d to 3s 6d a day for hewing and filling, twice a labourer's wage, but could not work more than five days a week. 'It would be too much'. Mr Wilson kept a night school at Nitshill, where he sometimes had 60 scholars, many of them married men. But for 16 years there had been no drawers in the school. 'They are wearied when they go home too much to attend school'. Drawers were the boys who pulled the coal from the face to the shaft. One of the drawers, Patrick Kinnon, aged nine, told Mr Tancred that he helped his brother in the pit. 'They come down to work about half past five: they get up again between four and five; do not go to school'. Two other drawers, Dennis Daily and his brother, aged 19 and 14, lived at Cross Arthurly and 'have to go and come to and from their work together about seven miles'.

There had been no serious accidents lately, but 36 years before there had been a very serious explosion in the Haugh pit when 18 people were killed: 16 funerals went away in one day to Paisley and two to Neilston. Peter Boag pointed out that in the Househill pit, which was so near that they could hear the men working in it, there had been many accidents, 32 or 33 people killed there in nine years, besides others injured.

Much worse was to come. Nine years after Tancred's visit, in the early hours of Saturday 15 March 1851, an explosion deep in the Victoria pit shook the village of Old Nitshill and the ground for a mile around. Sixty-one men and boys died more than a thousand feet underground. The tragedy occurred when the day colliers were about to relieve the night workers, and most of the trapped miners were in the north-west section of the pit near the Freetrader ventilation shaft. The first of only two survivors, John Cochrane, was not brought out until late on Sunday evening, and David Colville not until Monday. Both men were much exhausted, suffering from the freezing cold, and Colville severely burned about the face, neck and hands. They were taken home on stretchers, confined to bed and no one allowed to talk to them. A company of the 21st Infantry was despatched to assist the police in controlling the estimated crowd of 20,000 who gathered on Priesthill to watch the rescue. Teams of experienced colliers were quickly on hand from Dixon's colliery at Govanhill and Sir John Maxwell's at Cowglen and from the Haugh pit, but it was fully a week before the last body was recovered. The dead were put into coffins at the pit, taken home and then buried at St John's church in Barrhead and at the Abbey Church in Paisley. The official inquiry concluded that a tunnel had collapsed, cutting off the air supply and allowing gas to build up to dangerous levels. Ironically, ventilation in the pit was considered so good that a model of the pit had been made at a scale of a quarter inch to six feet ready for show at the Great Exhibition in London.

At the time of the disaster only persons born in the parish received poor relief, and most of the widows had been born in Ireland. A relief fund was set up for sufferers and dependants of victims, along with an additional fund to benefit the miners who had risked their lives in the rescue. Donations from the Earl of Glasgow and Messrs Coats of Paisley, owners of the pit, headed the list. A benefit in aid of the fund was held at the Prince's Theatre Royal in Glasgow, and the *Glasgow Herald* announced that two talented and popular artists would appear. Mr Mackay would play Dominie Simpson in a performance of *Guy Mannering* and Miss Isaacs would take the part of Maria in *The Daughter of the Regiment*.

Perhaps the most poignant record of the tragedy was made by James Thomson, whose painful duty it was to ennumerate the population for the National Census taken only two weeks after the disaster. In Old Nitshill, where the stricken community lived, the heads of 16 out of 50 neighhouring households are shown as 'widow - husband killed March 14, 1851, by an explosion at Victoria coal pit - living on charity'. (The date is incorrect.) Almost all the widows were between 20 and 40 years of age with young

Alum-calcining fields at Hurlet. The alum was prepared from shales taken from exhausted local coal wastes. The works were begun by Macintosh, Knox & Co in 1797 and were soon the largest in Scotland.

families. Betty Connelly, aged 23, had two children, Elizabeth and John, aged four and two; Betty Whitehouse, aged 24, was left to bring up Charlotte, Ruth and John, aged five, four and two; and Mary Mulholland, aged 25, was left with a year-old son, Henry, and an eight-day baby boy, named after his father, John, who died in the pit.

The Levern: a river beaded, as it were, with industrial establishments

As well as being rich in coal, the Hurlet seam contained copperas ore, found in the coal, and had a band of aluminous schistus above the coal. These two minerals could be used to produce copperas and alum, the principal mordants used in the dyeing process to fix colours, give them brilliance and make them durable. The manufacture of these substances became an early and important

This illustration shows boys washing the crystallised alum before it was crushed. Alum was used to fix dyes in the textile finishing industry.

industry at Hurlet and Nitshill.

The manufacture of copperas is believed to have been introduced into Scotland at Hurlet by John Lightbody of Liverpool in 1753, using the copperas stones, or pyrites, from the adjacent coal and lime work on the Hawkhead estate. Lightbody's works were on the site of the present Hurlet depot of the Renfrew Roads Department. The pyrites were first exposed, in heaps or on inclined beds, to the weather. After gradual decomposition and washing with rain water, this yielded a liquor, which on being concentrated by boiling, with a small addition of iron, produced green copperas, or sulphate of iron. This salt was used in making ink, in tanning leather and in dyeing the wool of hats black. Lightbody also attempted the manufacture of alum, but without success. The works were continued by Mrs Lightbody after her husband's death in 1791 and were bought over in 1820.

Alum was first successfully produced at Hurlet by the firm of Macintosh, Knox & Co in 1797 after experiments by Charles Macintosh — later of waterproof fame — had indicated that by the proper application of the principles of chemistry, alum could be successfully prepared from shales taken from exhausted coal wastes. The works were set up on a 20 acre field on the west bank of the Levern, on the site of the old Leggins pit. For an industrialist, Hurlet had the double advantage of a source of raw material at hand, and a ready market for the product at the printfields along the Levern at Corsemill, Barrhead, Fereneze and Neilston; at Pollokshaws on the Cart; at Thornliebank on the Auldhouse Burn; and at the field on the Brock Burn near Darnley operated by Charles Macintosh, Charles Tennant, James Knox of Hurlet and others. When Tennant and Macintosh moved their main operations to St Rollox in 1799, Macintosh's partner, John Wilson of Thornly, was left in charge of the Hurlet Alum Works. Similar works were started by Macintosh at Campsie in 1808 and the Hurlet and Campsie Alum Works became the largest in Europe.

After the deaths of Charles Macintosh in 1843 and his son George five years later, John King, who had begun as a clerk in the counting house at Hurlet, became owner of the company. In 1841 King went to reside at Levernholme on the east bank of the Levern, just above Hurlet. He later bought the Campsie estate, but did not break his ties with Levernholme where he died in 1875. His eldest son also began as clerk in the alum works and went on to become Sir James King, Lord Provost of Glasgow 1886–89. The firm was liquidated on the death of John King's son Robert in 1910 and Levernholme sold. It later became the home of Thomas Haywood Coats of the Paisley family. Glasgow Corporation acquired the house for an Old Folks Home and changed the name to Tinto House in honour of a former head of the Welfare Department. The house is now Glendale Nursing Home.

As well as coal and lime works, Messrs John Wilson & Sons had large scale chemical manufacturing interests at Hurlet and Nitshill. Wilson set up a second copperas work at Nitshill in 1807 which later became the Nitshill Chemical Works. In 1820 he purchased Lightbody's old copperas plant at Hurlet and began the manufacture of alum there with his son John as manager. By 1836 the company's annual output was 1,200 tons of alum at Hurlet and 300 tons of copperas at Nitshill plus an unspecified quantity of ironstone from their Hardfauld and other pits at Hurlet. This was in addition to output at their Haugh pit, which produced an annual 42,000 tons of coal, 5,000 tons of limestone and 6,000 tons of aluminous schist. At this date Wilson's workforce numbered 380 men in all, plus upwards of 40 horses, conveying the minerals and

The village shop at the Hurlet photographed in the 1930s. The shop stood at the north-west corner of the crossroads, and with the rest of the cottages has now disappeared.

other produce to Glasgow and Paisley. The Wilsons later had their own branch line to the Glasgow & Barrhead Railway.

The villages in the 1850s

In 1850 the Hurlet was a village of around 300 persons who lived around the junction of the road from Paisley to East Kilbride with the road from Barrhead to Glasgow. On the south-east corner there was a smiddy and a cooper's workshop. Archibald Renfrew was the master blacksmith, employing five other local men, and James Kennedy, the cooper, came from Kilmaurs. The adjacent row of single room houses were mostly occupied by alum workers. Several men were natives of distant parts of the Highlands such as Dornie, Tongue, Lochmaddy, Lochnagar, Banavie. Did Charles Macintosh employ a Gaelic speaking workforce at Hurlet to keep the process secret as his father had already done at the Cudbear Works begun in Duke Street in the 1770s? At the end of the row a path led down from Nitshill Road to the river at Levernshiels, a small community with another smiddy belonging to the Renfrew family. Waterwheel Row was a short row of houses sited between the river and the lade which came down from the cotton mill upstream. One of these houses functioned as a store.

East Hurlet House was built around 1763 and has recently been restored. A fine example of Scottish vernacular architecture.

On the north-west corner of the crossroads was another row of workers' houses curving round the foot of Hurlet Hill, with a store on the corner run by a local man, James Cunningham. The houses were occupied by coal miners, mostly Lowland Scots. At the west end of the row was Woodend Cottage, the home of James Hall, clerk of the alum works, and now demolished. Hurlet House, sometimes referred to as East Hurlet House, stood a little beyond the row on the north side. The house was reputedly built in 1763 and is a fine example of Scottish vernacular architecture. In the 1850s it was described as a superior dwelling house with offices and garden attached, the property of the Earl of Glasgow, held on lease by John Wilson & Sons and occupied by their manager John McBeath. Glasgow Corporation's plan in the 1970s to use the house for a museum of childhood was not carried through. The house has been well restored and is now a B-listed building in private ownership.

Next to Hurlet House is Roughmussel, presently occupied by the Parks and Recreation Department of Household District. This was formerly Roughmussel farmhouse. It was built around 1870 and occupied by James Motherwell as a replacement for the original farmhouse which stood on the opposite side of Barrhead Road, about the site of the present electricity sub-station. Roughmussel appears to have been a fairly small farm, about 40 acres, of the type noted in the *General Review of the Agriculture of Renfrewshire* as 'significantly described in the language of the county by the term *paffle*'. Richardson's map of 1795 gives the name as 'Rochmusch'. Between the earlier farmhouse and the Hurlet crossroads were another two rows of cottages known as Roughmussel Row and Watermally Row. These were occupied by Messrs Wilson's workers. West Hurlet House was the home of John Wilson of Thornly, partner of Charles Macintosh at the alum works and author of the *General Review* quoted above. In 1850 it was occupied by Dr Andrew Quinlin who attended at the Nitshill colliery disaster. The house remains in private ownership.

Nitshill in 1850 had a post office with two arrivals and despatches daily and a branch of the Western Bank of Scotland, open on Wednesdays and Saturdays for transacting business. A subscription school, the property of the school committee, stood at the top of Dunlop Street (now Dove Street), described as a commodious street, with William Brown the teacher. St Bernard's Primary now occupies the site. The village had two inns, the Wheat Sheaf Inn with 'good accommodation' managed by John Bennie, and the Nitshill Inn with 'moderate accommodation' run by Miss Ann Dove. Doves abounded in Nitshill. Archibald Dove was the village shoemaker, and Dugald Dove was quarry master and farmer of the 200 acre farm of Rosehill, just to the west of Peat Road, where a refurbishment scheme is taking place. Other traders included three grocers, a blacksmith, and a book vendor. The inns shown on the 1895 Ordnance Survey map of Nitshill are the Royal Oak Inn, the Railway Inn, and the Volunteer Arms. Pubs in 1995 are the Royal Oak, the Cavendish, the Levern Water Hotel and the Nia Roo (read it backwards).

In contrast to Hurlet, where the population did not greatly expand after the 1850s, Nitshill continued to grow, surging ahead after a station was opened on the Glasgow, Barrhead and Neilston Direct Railway in 1848, and reaching the one thousand mark in the 1860s. A report at that time states that the houses in New Nitshill were mostly newly erected buildings inhabited by miners and labourers. These were the 'rows' and 'lands' built by the various employers for their workforces: Pit Row, Blast Row, Smithy Row, Railway Row, Brick Row, Copperas Row, Dunlop's Land, Houdan's Land, White's Square and the Co-op Buildings.

Half way between Hurlet and Nitshill there was another small hamlet at Househillmuir, at the corner of the present Prestwick Street and Nitshill Road. The population of about 125 persons included William Anderson a cooper, who was also the letter receiver or sub-postmaster, and a grocer, tailor, joiner, and spirit merchant. Another small community of around 55 persons lived at Turnberry. This consisted of a miners' row and a line of villas then known as Household Cottages. The villas now form part of Glenlora Drive near Bankbrae Avenue. One of these houses was Household school and schoolteacher's house 'a pleasant ornamental building of two stories' erected and funded by the Misses Dunlop 'for the education of the inhabitants of Nitshill and neighbour-hood'. In the 1880s the other four houses, known as Gowanbank, Wellington Cottage, and two as Household Cottage, were occupied by a road surveyor, a colliery manager, an accountant, and Malcolm McPhail, a retired horse keeper from Oban. Gowanbank School on the hill above continues the name.

Howsle: a pretty dwelling and a reasonable good house

In 1750 Robert Dunlop, second son of James Dunlop of Garnkirk, purchased the Household estate and regained possession of lands which an ancestor had held for part of the 17th century. The old house or 'Place of Household' is described in 1710 as a 'neat and handsome dwelling' and another commentator of the same period, using the local pronunciation, says that 'Howsle' is 'a pretty dwelling and a reasonable good house'. The old house was replaced shortly after by a comfortable, modern mansion, which was probably the largest private house on the Levern.

James Dunlop, Colonel of the Renfrewshire Militia, succeeded his father in 1762. Coal mining was reported on the estate in the 1790s and by 1820 the family were also working extensive sandstone quarries. In a bid to secure the contract for supplying the stone to build the new cavalry barracks at Gorbals, Colonel Dunlop, as proprietor of the 'Nitshill' Stone Quarries, is recorded in the minutes of the Glasgow, Paisley and Ardrossan Canal Company in 1820 as negotiating preferential rates for transporting the 'principal stone, ashlar and rubble' from the wharf at Rosehill (Rosshall near Cardonald) to the terminus at Port Glasgow (presumably Port Eglinton). Dunlop claimed that the discount was necessary to offset the expense of carting the stone by road to the canal until the Hurlet railway he was constructing was ready for use. This was a horse-drawn waggon-way connecting his quarries at Old Nitshill with the canal. Its route was across the Household estate, along the west side of Crookston Road, then through a tunnel just before reaching the canal at Rosehill wharf.

After the death of their father in 1821, ownership of the Household estate passed to the four Misses Dunlop, Elizabeth, Janet, Harriet and Frances. Janet became a Mrs Campbell, and her three sisters continued to live on the estate until the 1850s. They then moved out of the 22 room mansion which had become 'almost unfit for occupation', leaving it to be occupied by the families of the workmen employed by Colin Dunlop & Co in their Nitshill Coal Company. Turnberry, Hartstone and Househillwood, former farm-steadings on the estate, were similarly occupied by workers. Frances, the last of the sisters, died in 1866 and the estate passed out of Dunlop family ownership five years later.

Hous'hill: Mrs Cochrane and Miss Cranston

William Stevenson, a farmer and quarrymaster, purchased House-hill House in 1872 and ownership remained with the Stevenson family until 1927, when it was sold to John Henderson, a Glasgow solicitor. Sadly, the house was severely damaged by fire in June 1934, allegedly caused by the heat of the sun's rays setting fire to woodwork under a glass-roofed dome on the upper floor. During this sad episode the cook sat under a tree weeping bitterly — a fire-engine had run over her foot. The house was eventually sold to Glasgow Corporation and demolished. The grounds are now covered by the Househillwood housing estate, but 60 acres have been made into a park on both sides of the Levern Water and include a children's play area on the site of the house.

The destruction of Household was a great loss, because it had been for the first two decades of this century the home of Miss Kate Cranston, owner of the renowned city tea-rooms. In 1904 Miss Cranston gave Charles Rennie Mackintosh a commission to completely decorate and furnish her residence as he had her tea-rooms. The fittings were destroyed in the fire, but many items of furniture were saved, and sold at auction in Glasgow in May 1933. Since then, most of them have disappeared. Fortunately photographs have survived. Two rooms at Hous'hill (as Miss Cranston liked to call the house) were especially note-worthy: the billiard room, because that was the only domestic billiard room by Mackintosh

Househill House, photographed by Annan around 1870. Miss Kate Cranston, of tearoom fame, later owned the house, and had it decorated and furnished by Charles Rennie Mackintosh.

which was actually executed; and the music room, which was visually divided from the drawing-room by an ingenious and very graceful semi-circular open screen. Quite astonishing was Mackintosh's audacity in creating a white bedroom at Hous'hill. This 'gentleman's retreat' was, after all, only a few hundred yards downwind of the alum works, the asbestos factory and the gas works. Hous'hill has been described as having 'arguably the best of Mackintosh's white bedrooms'. But it was also virtually his last white room and the last occasion on which he used white enamel on his furniture.

Kate Cranston married John Cochrane in 1892 when she was in her early forties. Cochrane was Provost of Barrhead and the First Lady was known locally as 'Kate o' the Big Hoose'. Provost Cochrane was proprietor of the Grahamstone Foundry and Boiler Works and is reported in the *Annals of Barrhead* as having neglected his foundry as a result of being drawn into Glasgow's artistic set. Sir Edward Lutyens wrote to his wife from the Buchanan Street tea-rooms:

> Miss Cranston is now Mrs Cochrane, a dark, fat wee body with black sparkling luminous eyes, wears a bonnet garnished with roses, and

has made a fortune by supplying cheap clean goods in surroundings prompted by the New Art Glasgow School.

Robert Grier, a stable boy at Househill from 1911–13, later gave his reminiscences of that time. 'It was Mrs Cochrane at Househill and Miss Cranston in the tea-rooms.' He remembered Mrs Cochrane as a kind and caring woman, but she was also very business like, a proper business woman. 'She aye put me in mind of Queen Victoria.' Robert's day began at half past seven when he had to help groom and harness the two horses, Britannia and Brutus, which took Mr and Mrs Cochrane to business in the brougham. Mr Cochrane dropped off at Barrhead and Mrs Cochrane took the train from Pollokshaws to Glasgow. Twice a week it was young Robert's task to drive a donkey cart from Househill to Glasgow, laden with plants, flowers and fresh vegetables for the various restaurants. The donkey was called Peggy, and Mrs Cochrane always had sugar lumps for the beast and a hot mid-day meal in the Argyle Street restaurant for Robert.

After her husband's death Mrs Cochrane left Househill to live for a number of years in the North British Hotel in George Square, and died in 1934 at Pollokshields.

The wider community

The interwar years saw the beginning of vast changes in the area. The Nitshill collieries had been in decline for many years and did not reopen after the General Strike of 1926. With unemployment reaching 70%, many people left the area. In 1926 the Glasgow City boundaries were extended to include both Hurlet and Nitshill, since when the district has seen the steady building of local authority housing over former farmland around the two villages.

In the interwar period two schemes were built, Nitshill and Househillwood. The Nitshill scheme was begun in 1932 at Mount Salterland on the south side of Nitshill Road and consisted of a mixture of four in a block and tenement housing. An extensive refurbishment of these houses has been carried out in the Pinmore Street area. Before 1932 the only buildings here were Nitshill Church and manse, both now demolished, and four older villas which still stand in Buchanan Terrace at the north end of Pinmore Street. The Househillwood scheme began in 1935 on farmland on the north end of the Househill estate. At the same time, the Peat Road, the old parish road which led to Old Nitshill from the north,

The Nitshill housing scheme was begun after the area became part of Glasgow in 1926. These houses in Pinmore Street have recently been refurbished.

was widened as far as Brock Road and Hartstone Road, the southern limits of the scheme. Peat Road was later realigned to form the main north-south dual carriageway through the area from Pollok Centre to Nitshill Road.

Close on the heels of Househillwood came Old Pollok, completed just before the outbreak of war in 1939. The ground had been sold to Glasgow Corporation for housing by Sir John Stirling-Maxwell on the understanding that they would build 'a garden-suburb superior even to Mosspark'. Old Pollok was always considered definitely up-market. As one resident put it, 'In Old Pollok we had chrome taps, in Househillwood they only had brass ones'. Househillwood, however, won hands down for their strong community spirit. Post-war building recommenced with South Pollok, a small scheme between Old Pollok and Househillwood, with German prisoners of war digging the trenches for the pipes and foundations. This scheme became one of the most notorious places in the district, known as the 'Bundy', gangland rhetoric for 'Boys United Never Die Young'. The Bundy was pulled down in the 1970s to make way for the Pollok Shopping Centre, opened by Princess Margaret in 1979 with the creation of around 600 jobs.

St Robert Bellarmine church in Peat Road was opened in 1959 to replace a smaller church built in 1942.

The next scheme was Craigbank, started on the remaining portion of the Househill estate in 1947. A unique feature here was the experimental central heating system, which was both expensive for the tenants and noisy. 'If you wanted to annoy someone, you tapped the pipes and it rattled through the whole building'. Craigbank also had a strong sense of community. The residents ran their own news-letter, the *Craigbank Bulletin*. Unfortunately the bowling greens, tennis courts and putting green at Newfield Square, at the south end of the scheme are no longer in use. The building in the centre of the square is used by the YMCA. Priesthill was started at the same time as Craigbank, but with 2,000 tenants drawn from different parts of Glasgow, it never achieved the social cohesion of other schemes. The name Priesthill is very old. It is mentioned in a document of 1563 granting the 20 shilling land of 'Priestishill', belonging to the Chapel of St Ninian at Darnley, to Sir John Stewart of Minto.

In the 1950s about 200 local authority houses were built at Hurlet on the former Roughmussel farmland. The last large housing scheme in the area was South Nitshill, bounded by Nitshill Road and Parkhouse Road. This was begun in 1957 on the former Darnley estate which was taken into Glasgow in 1938. The area includes the Darnley Industrial Estate.

When the new housing schemes were built, provision had to be made for churches and schools. The first Catholics in Hurlet and Nitshill attended St John's church in Barrhead or, after 1906, could attend mass in St Bernard's school or Nitshill public hall. At the end of 1941 a new parish was formed, dedicated to St Robert Bellarmine, the 16th-century Jesuit teacher canonised only eleven years previously by Pope Pius XI. A church was built and opened in May 1942, but soon proved too small for the growing population. The present church in Peat Road was opened in May 1959 by the Archbishop of Glasgow and the congregation is now one of the largest in the Diocese. This was the last church built by the firm Pugin & Pugin and there is a fine west window showing scenes from the life of the Saint. In 1949 St Conval's at Pollok was founded from St Robert's and in 1960 St Bernard's at South Nitshill, Bellarmine Secondary School was opened in 1962.

In 1940 Nitshill Church of Scotland, which had begun in 1844 as a Free Church, united with Levern Parish Church, and the Nitshill buildings in Pinmore Street were demolished. The Church of Scotland built a hall-church in Dove Street at Nitshill and this is now a linked charge with Priesthill. Priesthill was begun as a church extension charge in 1949 and a hall-church was dedicated in 1952 in Freeland Drive. A new church building was added in 1973, most of the cost being met from the sale of the Park Church at Lynedoch Place in Glasgow. This church was sold for office development on condition that the tower should be preserved and it is now a landmark in the Park area. Services are held in Priesthill and the Nitshill church is used as a meeting place for church organisations and other community groups. Other places of worship are Pollok Baptist Church in Haughburn Road and Priesthill Congregational Church in Houshillwood Road.

Lest we forget

Nitshill War Memorial, which stands near the station, is a granite column imaginatively decorated with Pictish and Celtic art forms, including interlacing, grotesque animals, and warriors on horseback. Among the names at the base is that of John Meikle MM, VC. John Meikle's family moved from Kirkintilloch to Nitshill in 1901 and John enlisted in the 4th Battalion Seaforth Highlanders in 1915 when he was only 16 years old. Like many others he almost

Memorial to Sergeant John Meikle, MM VC, in Station Square, Dingwall. John Meikle was a clerk at Nitshill Station, enlisted in the Seaforth Highlanders in 1915, and was one of the youngest Scots to be awarded the Victoria Cross.

certainly gave a wrong age. He served in France and won the Military Medal at Ypres in 1917, afterwards being promoted to Sergeant. John Meikle was awarded the Victoria Cross posthumously for his part in wiping out a machine gun nest during the Battle of the Scarpe on 20 July 1918. He was the only one of his Battalion to win the award during the First World War and one of the youngest Scots to win the Victoria Cross. John Meikle attended Levern School and was a clerk at Nitshill station. A granite memorial was erected in his honour on Nitshill station but sadly had to be removed in 1971 to protect it from vandalism, and it was re-erected in Station Square at Dingwall. In 1957 the school honoured its hero by incorporating a representation of the Victoria Cross in the school badge.

In December 1991 the Nitshill Mining Disaster Memorial was unveiled beside the War Memorial by Mrs Rose McCloy in memory of the 61 miners from the Victoria Pit who lost their lives on 15 March 1851. The memorial was erected with donations from the local community, traders, trade unions and Glasgow City Council.

Local landmarks which have disappeared include the Nitshill Village Hall which was built in the centre of the village in 1905 by public subscription with contributions from the local mine-owner, miners themselves and individuals. The hall was the focal point of community activities such as the Nitshill village choir. It survived the closure of the pits in the interwar period and for some time operated as a dance-hall, then as a cinema and during the war was frequented by the American servicemen billeted at Cowglen. The hall was latterly used as a Bookies. The money realised from the sale of the building was disbursed to pensioners at Christmas and through donations to schools. There is now a tenants' hall at Seamill Street. The Priesthill tenants' hall in Glenmuir Drive has recently been refurbished and offers a variety of classes, with aerobics for Senior Citizens very popular.

In 1980 the Local Plan for the area stated that Nitshill central area consisted of a mix of industry, housing and shops, and that though run down, 'the small scale variety and pedestrian bustle on Nitshill Road gives it the feel of a traditional small town centre'. Since then attention has focused on the refurbishment of the area without loss of community spirit and identity. The building of a sheltered housing unit at the corner of Dove Street and Nitshill Road keeps older people in the heart of the community and other projects like the Mitre project have provided care for the mentally handicapped. Nitshill's only tower block opposite the station is not too intrusive and is attractively decorated. Recent developments are the extensive refurbishment of flats in the Pinmore area and the building of private houses in a development to be called Glenmuir village.

At Hurlet the community expanded in the 1970s when around 100 houses were built for private ownership, but few traces of the old village remain. The newly opened Hurlet Inn at the crossroads is a family inn with children's play areas indoors and outdoors

The War Memorial at Nitshill is decorated with Pictish and Celtic art forms. Across the road is the only tower block in Nitshill.

and well suited to provide a focal point for the community. The neighbourhood is now known as Roughmussel. But it is pleasing that along with Hurlet House the inn will perpetuate the traditional name of the Hurlet.

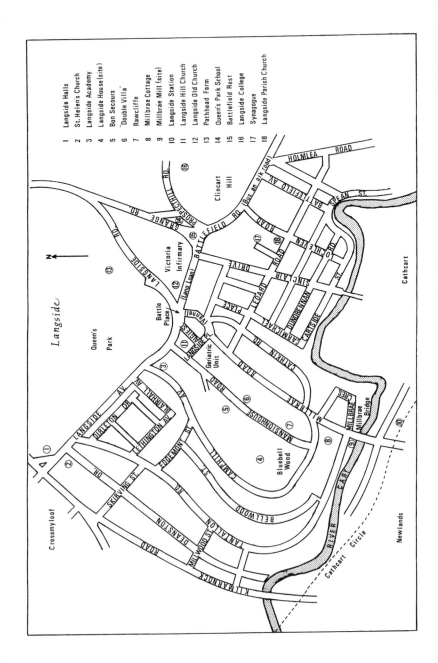

1 Langside Halls
2 St. Helen's Church
3 Langside Academy
4 Langside House (site)
5 Bon Secours
6 'Double Villa'
7 Rawcliffe
8 Millbrae Cottage
9 Millbrae Mill (site)
10 Langside Station
11 Langside Hill Church
12 Langside Old Church
13 Pathhead Farm
14 Queen's Park School
15 Battlefield Rest
16 Langside College
17 Synagogue
18 Langside Parish Church

CHAPTER 7
LANGSIDE

'Langside', wrote Crawfurd dismissively in 1710, 'a place only memorable for the defeat given to Queen Mary's troops, by those of her son King James VI under the command of James, Earl of Murray, Regent, 1568'. A century later, however, Langside was being extolled as an ancient village containing from 20 to 30 families, set down in a commanding situation, amid its fine little gardens on an eminence, 'overlooking a great expanse of cultivated country at hand, and high towering mountains in the distant view'. The little weaving community strung along the ridge of the hill had become a favourite destination for ramblers from Glasgow keen to escape for a few hours the noise and smoky breath of the city.

It was doubtless this commanding situation which influenced Thomas Brown to purchase around 120 acres of the lands of Langside in 1776 to form an estate and erect a mansion house on the splendid site. In 1852 the estate was sold by his grandson to Neale Thomson, proprietor of the adjoining Camphill estate. Thomson feued the Langside estate for cottages and villas, and the Camphill estate eventually became part of the Queen's Park. The development of this 'rising new suburb' was undoubtedly stimulated by the opening of Langside Station on the Cathcart Circle in 1894 and the introduction shortly after of electric tramcars.

The old village survived the era of villa development relatively unscathed, but was swept away by the tide of tenement building which began in Algie Street and Langside Place in 1895. One commentator wrote:

> The eight houses that remain of the score or so which formed the village at the middle of the century will soon have gone the way of their companions. They form one side of the narrow street, running directly south from the monument. The other side has disappeared, to be recreated shortly into red-stone tenements, and two huge derricks preside over the unsightly disorder of a builders' yard.

Tenement building spread to the low-lying ground to the east of Langside village and by the 1920s a grid of tenements reached as far south as the edge of the river Cart to form the new suburb of Battlefield. The increase of population brought to the district new churches and schools, the synagogue and other public buildings and institutions, stretching from Langside Hall on the west to Langside College on Clincart Hill on the east.

The Battle of Langside

The Battle of Langside was fought on 13 May 1568, eleven days after Queen Mary's escape from Lochleven Castle, during which interval the Queen was at Hamilton mustering a force of around 6,000 men. Regent Moray was meanwhile in Glasgow. Learning on the morning of the 13th that Mary was marching from Hamilton to Dumbarton by way of the south bank of the Clyde, Moray quickly moved his forces across the Clyde to take up a strong position on the high ground of Langside Hill, leaving the Queen to draw up her troops, under the command of the Earl of Argyll, on the lesser summit of Clincart Hill half a mile to the east, while she herself withdrew to watch the battle from Cathcart Hill one mile to the south.

The Queen's army attacked first. Protected on the right by their cavalry under Lord Herries, the van, composed mainly of Hamiltons, proceeded along the Bus an' Aik (bush and oak) road and charged up the Lang Loan (both now incorporated into Battlefield Road) to engage the Regent's right wing positioned at Langside village at the top of the hill. Mary's foot soldiers suffered heavy losses from Moray's hagbutters firing their guns from behind the protection of the hedges of the village gardens. Reinforcements summoned by Kirkcaldy of Grange from the Regent's left wing, drawn up behind Pathhead Farm, then joined in driving the Queen's troops back downhill into the path of her main force. Meanwhile the Regent's archers and then his cavalry, placed between the two wings of his army, moved downhill to rout Mary's horse and within three quarters of an hour the battle was over and the Queen's army was in full flight. Mary is traditionally believed to have left Cathcart by way of Mal's Mire Lane towards Rutherglen to begin her long flight south to England and captivity. Mary's losses have been estimated at over 100 slain and over 300 taken prisoner, while Moray lost few of his 4,000 men.

Queen's Park is called after Mary and many streets in the district are named for persons or places associated with the Queen:

The Monument to the Battle of Langside was erected in 1887 on the 300th anniversary of Queen Mary's death. The former Free Church, designed by local architect Alexander Skirving, is now a restaurant.

Grange, Carmichael, Dundrennan, Lochleven, Arundel and Craigmillar are all at Battlefield; Lethington, Dirleton, Blairhall and Tantallon at Langside; Herries, Kirkcaldy, Carberry and Darnley in Pollokshields; and Niddrie, Nithsdale, Moray Place and Regent Park Square at Strathbungo. Killigrew Road at Titwood and Mariscat Road at Pollokshields are named after two personalities at Mary's court; Sir Hugh Killigrew the English ambassador and 'Mariscat' a Court Jester.

In 1887 a memorial to the battle was erected at the top of Langside Hill on the 300th anniversary of Mary's death. The tall granite column stands in the centre of Battle Place on ground artificially heightened and is carved with thistles, roses and fleur-de-lis. The monument was restored by the Cathcart Society and others as part of Glasgow's 'Adopt a Monument Scheme' in 1988. From the top, a lion with his paw on a cannon ball looks eastward over the battlefield, much of it now covered with the buildings of the Victoria Infirmary . The Infirmary was opened in 1890 by the Duke of Argyll, descendant of Mary's commander. In 1894 things were evened up when the 15th Earl of Moray, descendant of the Regent, laid the foundation stone of Langside Free Church, later

143

known as Langside Hill. A pediment sculpture, intended to show John Knox remonstrating with the Queen, was never executed. After standing empty for several years, the former Free Church has been tastefully restored and reopened as 'The Church on the Hill' a bar restaurant purveying extensive food, real ale and foreign beers all day for seven days a week.

The monument and the Free Church were both the work of local architect Alexander Skirving. 'Sandy' Skirving was Alexander Thomson's chief draughtsman and the church follows Thomson's classical style, making an interesting contrast with the Gothic architecture of Skirving's earlier Langside Old Parish Church, which stood at the junction of Langside Road and Battlefield Road from 1888 until destroyed by fire in 1982. Chestnut Cottage, one of a row of seven villas on Langside Avenue facing the park, was the Skirving family home, demolished in the 1970s. Skirving Street, off Kilmarnock Road, perpetuates the name. Langside Library has a mural painting in the Children's Department of *The Battle of Langside* by Maurice Grieffenhagen ARA, 1919, gifted by the governors of Glasgow School of Art.

Langside village: apples, gooseberries and radical opinions

'It hing as it grew' was the phrase generally used to describe the village of Langside. However, the Ordnance Survey map of 1859 shows a regular pattern of about 20 houses, facing each other across a single village street (now Algie Street). The description may have applied to the 'Cruikit Raw', an irregular crescent of thatched cottages which at an earlier date guarded the entry to the village on the north side where Smiley's garage now stands. The map shows regular strips of ground behind the houses, liberally decorated with tree symbols, representing no doubt the famed apple trees and gooseberry bushes, the excellence of which during July and August tempted numerous parties from the neighbouring city. Glasgow folk used to come out for 'grossets' served from the bush and washed down by curds and cream and new milk. 'Apples, gooseberries and extreme radical opinions were what the weavers cultivated in their spare time.'

There were two entrances into Langside village. Using modern names, these were directly into Algie Street from Battle Place, or along the north part of Millbrae Road, then known as the Vennel, and into Langside Place from the east. Langside Place did not

A sketch of Millbrae made around 1827 showing the mill buildings in the foreground on different levels of the steep slope. The mill was destroyed by fire in 1848. A new bridge over the Cart was built in 1899.

extend west of Algie Street, and the south end of Algie Street was bounded by the grounds of the Langside estate. The second approach by the Vennel was preferred by ramblers who could then stop at the 'Refreshment Rooms' at Middlebank House, run by Janet Finlay and her son Matthew, the pastry baker. In the 1890s John Shand set up his carriage hire and funeral service business from Middlebank and his stables still exist behind Smiley's garage. Middlebank is one of the few surviving old houses in Langside village. The finest views over the surrounding countryside were also to be had from the Vennel, especially at Burnstyle farmhouse which stood at the corner of Millbrae Road and Langside Place with fields extending right down to the river Cart. In 1875 an outbreak of typhoid affected 13 children and three servants in six of the 'villa residences' in Langside. This was blamed on milk from infected dairies at Eaglesham. In the village proper of Langside, however, where the milk came from the local farm, there was not a single case of illness. The farmhouse became a dairy until the 1950s when it was demolished to make way for the Victoria Geriatric Unit.

New flats at Langside Gardens on the site of Langside House, home of the Browns of Lanfine and Langside.

It is not known when weaving began at Langside, but cotton handloom weavers headed 19 of the 24 households recorded in the village in 1841. Only six weavers remained in 1861 and all had disappeared by 1871. In 1895, Marion Kerr, who had lived in the village for 30 years, stated that the original feuars were called Algie, Thomson and Auld, and that the old houses had been built around 1710. Mrs Kerr remembered the small green on the south side of the village which the children used as their playground and where their elders played quoits. This was where the local boys were taught swordmanship by the veteran John Smith, who had fought at Corunna and had a sabre wound across his shoulder. Sergeant William Paton had fought at Waterloo and Andrew Gray, the village Hercules, was in the Crimea. In days long past, Mr Ronald, a West India sugar merchant, had experimented with a cane-cutting machine on kale stalks on the green. It was voted so efficient that it was sent out to the Indies. Mr Ronald occupied Queen Mary Cottage at the north end of the village. This house was later occupied by the land surveyor and map maker, William Kyle. According to Mrs Kerr, a Mrs Thomson who lived in the village was Betty Burns, daughter of the poet and Anna Park.

Another small community existed at Langside Meal Mill, about half a mile south of Langside village. The mill stood on the west side of the bridge over the Cart, with the mill wheel at the corner of what is now Tantallon Road. The mill was destroyed by fire in 1848, and only the miller's house survived. This is the cottage which stands on the slope of the hill, looking over the site of the mill to Millbrae Bridge and Newlands beyond. The mill was a large affair, and had two roads to it at different levels. One led to the granary, and the lower one to the 'killogie' or firing-house, where pease etc were dried. The lengthy mill lade left the river at the bend near Battlefield Avenue, turned east to pass under Carmichael Place , then south again along Millbrae Crescent and had its outlet a short distance above Millbrae Bridge. This low-lying area is still prone to flooding despite the efforts of the White Cart Flooding Association set up in 1990.

The Browns of Langside

The Browns of Langside, and later also of Lanfine in Ayrshire, owned the Langside estate from 1776 to 1852. Thomas Brown, the son of Nicol Brown, a surgeon in Newmilns of Loudoun, pur-chased Langside when he was about 46 years of age and died there six years later in 1782. Thomas was succeeded by his sons George and Robert who both died unmarried. Their brother, Thomas Brown MD, born in 1774, a distinguished physician and surgeon at Glasgow Royal Infirmary, inherited Langside in 1841. Dr Brown sold the estate eleven years later, just one year before his death in March 1853.

Shortly before his death, Dr Brown, with the assistance of his daughter, Miss Martha Brown, wrote a memoir entitled *All About the Family, by T. Brown, Jany. 1853, in the 79th year of his age*. This is a valuable account of his father's adventures as a young man and life on the Langside estate around 1780.

It is clear that the first Thomas Brown's early life was not only adventurous, but also profitable. After completing his classical and medical studies at Glasgow University, Thomas went to sea as a ship's surgeon, making the first of four or five voyages to India and China when he was 22 years old, and taking the chance to trade on behalf of his brother John, of the firm of Brown, Carrick & Co, bankers and cotton merchants in Glasgow. Having realised a moderate fortune, Thomas then settled as a surgeon apothecary in London, where he married Martha Bogle, of the Glasgow merchant family. In 1775 the Browns made the 14-day journey back to Glasgow with their young family. Thomas became a partner in the Ship Bank with his brother and other gentlemen and within a few years was drawing an annual income of £660 from the bank.

According to the memoir, Thomas Brown bought the Langside estate for 'above £4,000, and had a handsome and expensive mansion house built there'. The house was 'from a plan of that eminent architect Robert Adams, an intimate friend of my Father and Mother'. Photographs show Langside House as a spacious classical mansion, three stories high, with adjoining offices forming courtyard on the north side. The memoir recalls the glittering parties of the 1780s:

> My mother when dressed for a party wore a hoop; and I recollect well that even my sister Marianne, tho' at that time under ten years of age, was on these occasions dressed in a similar manner. She also had a hoop. My father of course wore powder, pomatum, and a long queue. I think he wore a cocked hat. I recollect quite well that he had a red embroidered waistcoat with silver buckles at his knees and buckles on his narrow pointed shoes. My mother had sharp pointed shoes with high heels and with buckles. In these days we had no umbrellas.

Dr Brown relates how his father began to lay out the garden and grounds and add to the wood at Langside. This was a natural wood of 24 acres which had about 30 or 40 years before been cut as a copse wood, but the oak and birch had regrown to a respectable size. Although only $2^1/_2$ miles from Glasgow, the wood contained a great number of foxes and jays. 'Our poultry suffered very naturally'. At that time the nests of the jays were very frequent, but now, in 1853, remarks Dr Brown, they are seldom seen, for 'the enormous bustle of Glasgow has for a long time eradicated the wild animals from its neighbourhood'. Dr Brown makes no mention of the impressive boulder with Bronze Age cup and ring markings now on display in the Kelvingrove Museum with the caption 'found prior to 1902 in the Blue Bell Wood to the south of Langside House'.

The children were educated at home by tutors and Robert and Thomas followed their father to Glasgow University. Thomas went on to a distinguished career, a graduate of both Glasgow and Edinburgh, and admitted to the Faculty of Physicians and Surgeons of Glasgow in 1799. Dr Thomas Brown was also a popular lecturer in botany at Glasgow University from 1799 to 1816, attracting a class of 55 students in 1810. His teaching methods required large numbers of flowering plants for demonstration and examination, and each student was issued with a specimen of all the plants under discussion. The College Physic Garden was in a poor state by that time, neglected and affected by smoke from factory chimneys. Brown called it 'that plot of ground which is dignified with the name of Botanic Garden'. The gardener was despatched to collect the necessary plants where he could. 'Oftentimes' he wrote, 'I have travelled to a wood or waterside two or three miles from town' and this description very aptly fits the Brown family estate. The College accounts record that in 1733 two College gardeners were paid 12 shillings Scots for going to Langside Woods in search of twigs to make besoms for sweeping the cut grass and clover on the walks of the College Garden.

Thomas Brown left his large collection of minerals, rocks, fossils and antiquities to be shared after his death between the Universities of Glasgow and Edinburgh. A selection of these are displayed in the Hunterian Museum and a portrait of Thomas Brown by Colvin Smith hangs outside the Randolph Hall. The Lanfine collection rates among the top five mineral collections in the United Kingdom. Dr Brown was ahead of his time by forming his collection from material he collected himself locally, for example in the Kilpatrick Hills, as well as by purchases from dealers. Dr Brown's daughter Martha bequeathed to Glasgow University in 1902 the sum of £5,000 for the Lanfine Bursaries in Arts.

After the elder Thomas Brown's death in 1782, the mansion house appears to have been let, but the family continued to spend their summers at Langside Cottage, a substantial house at the north end of the estate, adjoining the village. The Victoria Geriatric Unit now occupies the site of the Cottage. Among later occupants of the mansion house were Thomas Hill, Registrar of Sasines for Glasgow and Chairman of the Caledonian Railway Company, and Stephen Alley of the Sentinel Engineering Works in Polmadie. In the 20th century the estate was owned by a builder and contractor and part let out as a poultry farm. In the 1950s Langside House was used as a Preparatory School for St Aloysius and then finally demolished. The site has been developed with well laid out apartment blocks appropriately named Langside Gardens, set in the famous Bluebell Woods where the cratties still blossom by myriads in May.

Villa residences

The Langside estate was feued out in 1852 and the first villa completed four years later, was Alexander Thomson's 'Double Villa'. This is not a single villa, but two semi-detached houses now numbers 25 and 25a Mansionhouse Road. In his brilliant design, Thomson turned the plan of one house through 180° to make each facade asymmetrical and identical. The villa was originally called 'Mariaville' after the wife of the first owner, Henry Watson, a Fife clothier. No 25 with its entrance facing Mansionhouse Road was later renamed 'Strathairly' and its twin facing Millbrae Road, became 'Hilton'. The design is further unified by the low pitched roof and strong horizontal emphasis typical of Thomson's villas. A nearby terrace of houses at numbers 2–38 Millbrae Crescent are thought to have been completed after Thomson's death in 1875 by his partner, Robert Turnbull.

The 'Double villa' stood alone in Mansionhouse Road until Rawcliffe Lodge was built in 1862. Rawcliffe later became a Carmelite convent, with a modern chapel tastefully incorporated within the Victorian House. This was the home of Alexander Stewart, of the firm of Stewart and McDonald, drapery warehouse-men, whose premises occupied the site of Fraser's store on the corner of Buchanan Street and Argyle Street. The exuberant 'Balmorality' of Rawcliffe must have presented a formidable challenge to the classical simplicity and elegance of Langside House. On the wall to the right of the main entrance to Rawcliffe is a stone carving of a female head wearing a hat with a splendid ostrich feather, which must surely represent Stewart's wife, Fanny, who ruled over a household containing eight children, a governess and a retinue of 14 servants.

Alexander Ballantyne Stewart was chairman of the Glasgow Institute of the Fine Arts and Rawcliffe contained a large picture gallery, where guests could sit and chat round the capacious fireplace over an after-dinner cigar before inspecting the works of living artists hung on the walls and the collections of jewellery, illuminated manuscripts, old china, rare enamels and exquisite carvings in ivory displayed in cabinets in the gallery and through-

Alexander Thomson designed his 'Double Villa' as two identical semi-detached houses facing opposite directions. These were the first houses in Mansionhouse Road, erected in 1856.

out the house. Stewart cultivated orchids at Rawcliffe and grew flowers at his country house, Ascog Hall, on the Isle of Bute, where he was Flag Officer of the Royal Northern Yacht Club. Regattas in Rothesay usually finished with a fire-works display from Mr Stewart's steam yacht. A B Stewart died in 1880 at the early age of 34, but the family occupied Rawcliffe until 1919, when the house was converted into a convent by the Order of Carmelite Nuns.

Other villas on the east side of Mansionhouse Road are Moray Bank, now a home run by the Order of St John, and Kirklinton, once the residence of the locomotive builder, William Lorimer, and now the Boswell Hotel. Most of the villas on the west side now form part of Bon Secours Hospital, including no 32, Norwood, which was the home of Matthew Algie, tea merchant and member of the old Langside family, whose firm continues in business in Glasgow as 'the market leader in the supply of tea, fresh ground coffee and coffee brewing systems to the UK Hotel and Catering Industry'.

Many of the earliest occupants of the new villa suburb on the slopes of Langside Hill worked in the textile industry. Others were merchants trading to West India, South America, Africa and every corner of the Empire on which the sun never set. Their wives came from Grand Canary, Gibralter, Brazil, their children had been born in Cuba and Demerara, and their sons came home on visits from

Architectural details on buildings at Langside:
Top Left and Bottom: Rawcliffe: woman's head, probably Mrs Fanny
Stewart; monogram of A B Stewart and date 1862.
Top Right: Langside monument showing thistles, fleur-de-lis, roses.

Australia. The district was especially popular with grain merchants. John McDougall at Kinnoull Cottage was a corn factor (his wife was from Perth), and William Hay at Edington House was a flour miller from Hutton in Berwickshire. Several churches from within and outwith the parish had their manses in Langside, and the district was popular with professional men. Industrialists who arrived in the 1890s included William Lorimer and Stephen Alley, the locomotive builders, and Albert zum Bach, an exporter of coal and chemicals. After the turn of the century two jewellers, Philip Woolfson and James Mark, came to live in Mansionhouse Road.

The villas on the Battlefield side of the hill remain fairly intact, but on the west side of the hill, off Langside Avenue, three streets of large 1870s villas were replaced in the 1970s by blocks of apartments built for Strathclyde Housing Association. The apartments are of three or four storeys, off-set by taller eight storey blocks round the perimeter of the scheme, and the names of Lethington, Dirleton and Tantallon have been preserved. Another group of apartment blocks have been built on the south side of Camphill Avenue above Millbrae Mill. These replace the old villas known as Ashlee, Brampton and Beechwood. Two original villas, Hazelwood and Thornwood, remain on the north side of Camphill Avenue and are occupied by Marist Brothers.

Schools, churches and public buildings

With the arrival of the 'villa residences' came Langside Academy, established in 1858 by George Adam, a native of Aberdeen, who had previously taught at the Normal School at Cowcaddens. The Academy was housed in a handsome building designed by Alexander Thomson at the corner of Langside Avenue and Camphill Avenue. It fully lived up to its description in the school prospectus as built expressly as an Educational Establishment for Young Ladies and Gentlemen, and beautifully situated at the foot of Langside Wood, and well situated to promote the health of the pupils'. Edgehill House was later built adjacent to the Academy to accommodate boarders from both Scotland and overseas.

After the early death of George Adam, the school was run by his widow and family. Alexander Adam became Head Master, assisted by his brothers, Mr Thomas and Mr Hector, and his sister, Miss M Adam. Mrs Jane Adam, the Lady Principal, 'exercised a constant supervision of the Young Ladies, attending to their

153

manners and deportment in the upper half of the Institution, entirely separate from that of the Young Gentlemen and with separate play-ground and entrance'. Sergeant Robertson gave instruction in drill, fencing and calisthenics, defined as 'the art or practice of taking exercise for health, strength or grace of move-ment'. In the Upper School both boys and girls were prepared for Edinburgh University local examinations. Around 1900 the school appears to have changed hands and had a short existence as Langside Girls' High School, under a R J Baillie, before being demolished to make way for tenements.

The first public school established by the School Board of Cathcart was Queen's Park Elementary School which began in 1873 in a mission hut in Strathbungo with Leander Fyfe as sole teacher. A permanent school was built at Grange Road three years later with around 250 pupils and three teachers moving into 'Board', the first of the four buildings that were eventually to form Queen's Park School. The other buildings were South (completed in 1884), North (1902) and Mid (mid 1920s). Queen's Park became a Higher Grade school in 1900 and Infant and Junior pupils were moved in two stages (1907 and 1912) to a new Battlefield Primary School in Carmichael Place. Battlefield later became a Junior Secondary school and the buildings are now shared between Battlefield Primary and Cartvale Special School. Langside Primary was opened in 1906 with provision for 1,200 children under headmaster John Gilchrist, and remains in use in Tantallon Road. In 1967 the name Queen's Park was transferred to a new comprehensive school at Toryglen and the school finally ceased to exist in June 1994. The original buildings at Grange Road became a teachers' resource centre. North building was destroyed by fire in December 1995.

In summer 1994 a reunion was held to celebrate Queen's Park School's 121 year history and several well-known former pupils attended or sent greetings. The roll of former pupils includes Ian McCaskill, Tom Honeyman, Ally McLeod, Emanuel Shinwell, Winnie Woodburn (Winifred Ewing MEP), Sir Isaac Wolfson and Stanley Jefferson, alias Stan Laurel, who paid a return visit to his old school in the 1940s with Oliver Hardy and distributed sweeties.

Langside Parish Church is a new building to be opened in 1996 in Ledard Road on the site of the recently demolished church which was built by H E Clifford in 1909 as Battlefield Parish (later West) Church. Two other congregations are represented in the

Langside Academy, established in 1858 by George Adam, flourished for 40 years in Camphill Avenue. The Academy building on the left was designed by Alexander Thomson and was demolished to make way for tenements. Edgehill House on the right accommodated the family and boarders, and is now in private ownership.

present membership, Langside Old Parish and Erskine-Rose. Erskine-Rose Church stood in Cartvale Street, but had very old roots going back to two Gorbals churches, Erskine Old in South Portland Street and Rose Street in Florence Street.

Battlefield East Church at the corner of Battlefield Road and Cathcart Road was built by a Free Church congregation which held its first meetings in William Geddes's dye-works at Cathcart. The earlier of the two church buildings used by the present congregation was designed in 1865 by John Honeyman and now serves as the church hall. Services are held in the adjoining red sandstone church built by John Galt in 1912. The later church contains a fine window by the Glasgow artist Sadie McLellan, *Agony in the Garden*, installed in 1972. In 1979 Battlefield East was united with Langside Hill church, whose origins lie in a Free Church congregation which held its first services in Langside Academy and then worshipped in an 'unsightly brick building' across the road in Queen's Park, before moving up to Langside Hill in 1896.

St Helen's Church, at the corner of Langside Avenue and Deanston Drive, has served the Catholic community in Langside since 1966. The building was formerly Langside Avenue Church of Scotland which was united with Shawlands Old in 1963. Langside and Shawlands United Free Church is situated in Millwood Street, off Kilmarnock Road, and was formed in 1929 by members of Langside Hill and other United Free congregations in neighbouring districts who wished to remain outside the union with the Established Church. Services took place in Langside Hall until the church was built in 1934.

Throughout the 20th century Langside Hall has hosted a wide variety of functions, concerts and community activities. The hall was the former National Bank of Scotland building in Queen Street. It was removed stone by stone to Langside by the Corporation in 1901 and converted to public halls by the city engineer A B McDonald. The handsome exterior by John Gibson has remained almost intact. On top of the building is the Royal Coat of Arms, flanked by the statues of Peace and Plenty, and on the keystones representations of five British rivers, the Clyde, Thames, Severn, Tweed and Humber.

A caring community: the Deaf and Dumb Institution

Langside has several institutions devoted to the care of the sick, the handicapped, or other disadvantaged groups. The earliest was the Glasgow Society for the Education of the Deaf and Dumb, who moved its premises from the city centre at Parson Street to a new purpose-built building on Clincart Hill, designed by James Salmon, senior, and formally opened by the then Lord Provost of Glasgow on 22 May 1868. The move to a fresh air site was much overdue. Despite the efforts of Duncan Anderson, an outstanding headmaster, an early admission register from the city centre period shows many deaths from dropsy, typhus, cholera and especially consumption. By the early 1870s the roll at the new Institution had risen to about 90. The children were aged between seven and seventeen, and the staff were not much older. The new headmaster, John Thomson, his two assistant teachers (one deaf and dumb from birth), matron and her assistant, and the cook, laundress, tablemaid and two housemaids were in their twenties or younger. Isabella Coutts, the matron, later became Mrs John Thomson.

A new headmaster was appointed in 1891. This was William Addison, who had already held posts at Edinburgh, Liverpool, and Exeter, and who remained at Langside until his retirement in 1920. His log book gives a picture of the life of the school, in and out of the classroom. In 1891 the Inspectors expressed satisfaction with the course of instruction which embraced articulation and lip reading, language including composition and grammar, arithmetic, drawing and writing and spelling, mainly determined by the eye, and geography. Woodwork, clay-modelling, needlework and gymnastics were also taught. In September, Mr Haydock had just returned from a course at Naäs in Sweden. Outings for the pupils are noted: visit to Princess' Theatre to see Pantomime; pupils visited BB Picture House to see the film *Tarzan and the Apes*, visit much enjoyed and proved also very instructive. This was the Bright and Beautiful Cinerama, later the Odeon, in Victoria Road.

In 1918 staff and pupils celebrated the Jubilee of the move to Langside. As a treat the school went to the Theatre Royal to see a cinematic representation of Jules Verne's *20,000 Leagues under the Sea*, with a special tea afterwards. As 1918 was also the 350th anniversary of the Battle of Langside, the children visited the Queen Mary Relics Exhibition in Langside Library and found it 'very interesting'. The same year a party of children entertained the wounded soldiers in the YMCA hut at Stobhill Hospital. This was 'very successful' and the soldiers 'much interested'. In 1919 it was on with the celebrations for the Centenary of the founding of the Society, with a special service in Camphill UF Church with Mr Hansell interpreting, and a reunion of ex-pupils and friends. In 1920 the Institution and its 150 pupils were transferred into the care of the Glasgow Education Authority, and Mr Addison announced his retirement at the end of the year. His last days were business pretty much as usual. On 27 November, Archie McMillan fell in the playroom and dislocated his right elbow. 'Dr Macleod sent for and the elbow put right'. On 24 December Mr Addison sent the children home, paid the teachers' salaries to the end of the year, and on 31 December logged his last entry: 'Finished up as far as possible all matters preparatory to handing over control to the new Superintendent. Signed W. H. Addison, 31st December 1920'.

After the Second World War the building reopened in 1947 as Langside College of Further Education, offering general and vocational education for young people on a day-release basis, and a range of vocational subjects and leisure time activities in the evening. A new building was added in 1964 to meet the increased demand for technical education, and provide modern facilities such as a swimming pool, dining rooms, gymnasia and an assembly hall. The College continues the caring tradition through its Department of Social Caring and Community Studies.

A caring community: the 'Vicky', Bon Secours and the Gertrude Jackson Orphanage

In 1878 Dr Ebenezer Duncan, a general practitioner in Crosshill, convinced his colleagues in the Glasgow Southern Medical Society of the urgent need for a voluntary hospital on the south side of Glasgow, where one third of the city's 700,000 population lived. Fund-raising was interrupted by the collapse of the City of Glasgow Bank the same year and by delays in the payment of a bequest of £10,000 from the estate of William Dixon of Dixon's Ironworks and £40,000 from Robert Couper of Millholm. The Infirmary was eventually opened on St Valentine's Day, 1890. With the assent of the Queen, it was named the Victoria Infirmary and granted permission to display the Royal Arms above the entrance. On the stone above the Arms is the figure of a puma, the symbol of medical care, and the puma also appears on the badge awarded to student nurses on passing their examinations. The library stamp used by the hospital has a sketch of a puma done by Dr Osborne Henry Mavor, better known as the playwright James Bridie, who was a visiting physician at the Victoria for 18 years.

Dr Duncan, who disliked his first name and was known as 'Eben', became one of the first two visiting physicians and was still on the board of Governors at the time of his death in 1922. He is commemorated by a bronze plaque in the main entrance hall. It is said that Dr Duncan's residence, Queen's Park House, at the corner of Langside Road and Grange Road, was built as near as possible to the Queen's Park Bowling Club of which he was both president and champion. It is now the headquarters of the hospital management.

The original Infirmary building, with accommodation for 84 patients and 40 staff, was designed by James Sellars in the form of two pavilions at right angles to a central block. A third and fourth pavilion were added later, but only the last has retained the dis-

Part of the Victoria Infirmary, the South Side's largest hospital. Only one of the four pavilions has retained its original bowed end and five stories of balconies.

tinctive bowed end with its airy verandah overlooking Battlefield Road. In 1935 a new Nurses Home and an Outpatients' Department and Accident Centre were opened, the latter by Viscount Weir, whose family were among the Infirmary's benefactors.

Langside Cottage became the residence of the Medical Superintendent in 1912. Two outstanding administrators, Dr Duncan MacGregor, also founder of the X-Ray department, and Dr Bryce McCall Smith, held this post between 1900 and 1935. In 1971 a new purpose built geriatric unit was opened on the site of the demolished cottage. The unit was known locally as the 'Hilton', and was the first in Scotland specially designed for the care of elderly people, with 256 in-patient beds for patients recovering from strokes, or suffering coronary heart disease, chest infections or Parkinson's disease. The large day-hospital on the ground floor has facilities for physiotherapy, dentistry, chiropody and social work. The Victoria now has 475 beds with out-patient facilities. Southsiders still look on the 'Vicky' as their own hospital.

The Sisters of Bon Secours de Paris first came to Glasgow in 1948 and established a small nursing home for the elderly at Norwood in Mansionhouse Road. Bon Secours means 'Good Care' and the primary role of the Order is to care for the sick. In 1960 Bon Secours Hospital was built with 63 beds on the site of two adjacent villas on the west side of Mansionhouse Road to provide private medical care for patients of all religious creeds and none. Care is provided by Sisters of the Order and other nursing staff. Numbers 38 and 40 Mansionhouse Road have recently been converted into Langside Priory Hospital, a private acute psychiatric unit.

The provision of care has always been of importance for Langside's sizeable Jewish community. The Gertrude Jackson Orphanage was opened in 1913 in memory of the daughter of Joseph Jackson, in a house at 53 Millbrae Road, with space for 16 children. Six years later it moved to larger premises at no 6 Sinclair Drive, where there was accommodation for 40 children and spacious grounds, including a fruit garden. During the First World War groups of children from Belgium and later refugees from Austria and Hungary were given shelter in the home, until a larger children's hostel was built at Garnethill. The villa in Sinclair Drive then became the Habonim Youth Centre and is now a private nursery. A Hebrew congregation was formed for the Langside, Cathcart and Mount Florida area in 1906 and in 1915 Queen's Park Synagogue, the first to be built south of Gorbals, was opened in Lochleven Road. A larger Synagogue was built twelve years later in Falloch Road, and has become particularly noted for the 22 pictorial stained glass windows designed and installed between 1988 and 1992 by John K Clark. The artist has taken the symbolism of Jewish festivals throughout the year, and has created the final beautiful result by using techniques virtually identical to those used by medieval craftsmen.

For many years the Church of Scotland operated its Metro-politan Mission, a training centre for overseas missionaries, within the house that is now the Boswell Hotel. Glasgow Corporation ran a residential home at 73 Millbrae Road. Hanover House is a purpose built elderly complex in Sinclair Drive, on the site of the old Mayfair Cinema, and day care is provided at the David Cargill Club in Ledard Road.

The Battlefield Rest, once described as the most exotic tram shelter in Scotland, is now a restaurant. Shortly after this photograph was taken in September 1995, the former Queen's Park School buildings behind the 'Rest' were damaged by fire and only 'Mid' building has escaped demolition.

A unique 80 year old institution for the care and comfort of all, but especially for the travelling public, happily still survives more or less intact after 1,500 people signed a petition in 1983 to save it from destruction. This is the 'Battlefield Rest', built in 1915, a local landmark, a service station before its time, once described as the most exotic tram shelter in Scotland. Decorated with gleaming green and cream tiles, the 'Rest' had a kiosk at one end under the octagonal clock tower, and public conveniences at the other, and became a B-listed building in 1981. The 'Rest' has now been transformed into a restaurant and continental bistro.

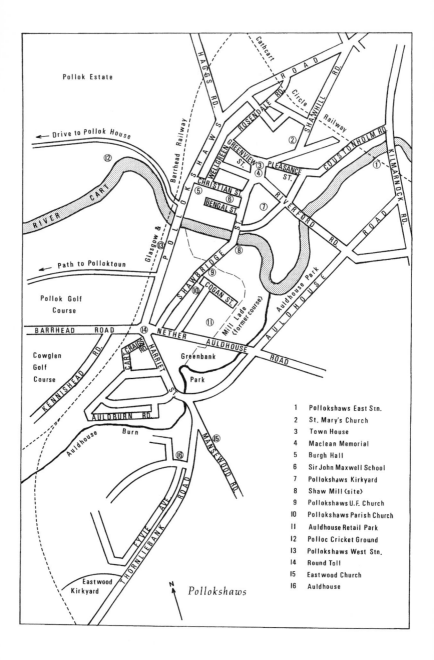

1   Pollokshaws East Stn.
2   St. Mary's Church
3   Town House
4   Maclean Memorial
5   Burgh Hall
6   Sir John Maxwell School
7   Pollokshaws Kirkyard
8   Shaw Mill (site)
9   Pollokshaws U.F. Church
10 Pollokshaws Parish Church
11 Auldhouse Retail Park
12 Polloc Cricket Ground
13 Pollokshaws West Stn.
14 Round Toll
15 Eastwood Church
16 Auldhouse

Pollokshaws

CHAPTER 8

POLLOKSHAWS

The name 'Poock Shawes' is shown on Timothy Pont's map published by Blaeu in 1654. 'Shaws' denotes woodland and 'Pollok' possibly comes from the Gaelic pol, a pool, as the White Cart flows here between much flat land or holms. Pollokshaws is also mentioned in 17th-century estate, legal and church records. 'John Wallace in Pollockshaws' testified against Sir John Maxwell in 1683 when Sir John was tried for high treason, accused of furnishing Presbyterian rebels and traitors with meat and drink in his own house. Neither Shaws nor Pollokshaws appears as a place name in the Poll Tax returns for Eastwood parish in 1695, but 15 years later Crawfurd briefly mentions 'the village of Pollockshaws, the property of Sir John Maxwell of Pollock, Bt; at which place there is a stone bridge of 2 arches over the river Cart'.

The village may have grown up round the meal mill on the left bank of the Cart beside the Shaw Bridge. Alternatively Pollokshaws may have developed at the Town Cross where the road from Glasgow to Irvine crossed the road from Govan to Cathcart. The earliest known date for a house in the village is 1623 on a lintel found during demolition near the old Town House. In the Examination Roll prepared in 1708 for the minister of Eastwood parish, Pollokshaws is divided into three districts. By far the greatest part of the population live in Pollokshaws proper, extending from the Shaw Bridge northwards to Shawhill and from the Cow Loan (later Pollok Street and now Greenview Street) eastwards via the Pleasance to the bank of the Cart at Coustonholm. Immediately to the south of the Shaw Bridge the district is called Bogle's Bridge, where only 20 persons are listed, and still further south at Harriet Street is a third village, Auldhouse. There are 36 persons on the roll at Auldhouse Bridge and Auldhouse House. Children under the examinable age of 12 years are excluded. Separate names were still in use for these three villages through the 18th century and were still used when Pollokshaws was erected into a Burgh of Barony in 1813 with a population of almost 3,000.

Auldhouse is a 17th-century mansion house, now said to be

Glasgow's second oldest house. The oldest part, the crow-stepped L-shaped block, was probably built by George Maxwell of Auldhouse, minister of Mearns, or by his son John, minister of Eastwood and the High Church of Glasgow. The lintel over the fireplace has the date 1631 and the inscription:

THE BODIE FOR THE SAUL WAS FRAMD: THIS HOVS THE BODIE FOR:
IN HEAVNE FOR BOTH MY PLACE IS NAMD IN BLISS MY GOD T'ADOR

In more recent times Auldhouse became a Children's Home. It has now been restored and converted into flats and new houses have been built on part of the ground.

From the mid 18th-century Pollokshaws was increasingly an industrial community of great diversity, although textile manufacture dominated. The Burgh escaped annexation to Glasgow until 1912 when the population was estimated at around 13,000. The Shaws has managed to keep its distinctive character despite Glasgow's redevelopment plan of 1958 which obliterated most of the old landmarks and replaced them by the high flats which tower over the main street and the White Cart river.

The Maxwell family and Pollokshaws

The Maxwell family is believed to have settled at Pollok before the middle of the 14th century. A branch of the family, the Maxwells of Nether Pollok, were given a charter of their lands in 1494. There are thought to have been three successive castles in the area before the present Pollok House was built in the 1740s, but their exact whereabouts are uncertain. The lands were lost by Sir John Maxwell who supported Mary Queen of Scots at Langside, but were returned by James VI in 1584. The following year Sir John began to build Haggs Castle to replace the Laigh Castle, by then in disrepair. The Nether Pollok lands later passed to other branches of the family, the Maxwells of Auldhouse, the Maxwells of Blawarthill, then the Stirling-Maxwells.

The first of the Auldhouse branch to become the laird of Nether Pollok was Sir George Maxwell, the son and grandson of the staunch Presbyterian ministers who built Auldhouse. Like many men of his time, Sir George was zealous in his pursuit of witches, and took part in a witch trial at Gourock in 1676. Shortly after, Sir George was himself bewitched, taken ill with a 'hot and fiery distemper' and for seven weeks suffered great pains, 'chiefly on the right side'. Following information from a dumb girl recently

A view over Pollokshaws to the north. As part of the redevelopment plan of the 1960s, the old village was swept away and around twenty high flats were built, including those at Shawbridge (left) and Shawhill (right).

come to live on the estate, effigies of Sir George with pins in their sides were found at the house of Janet Mathie, widow of the under miller at the Shaw Mill. Janet Mathie, her son John Stewart 'a warlock in Pollokshaws', her daughter Annabel and three other unfortunate women were arrested, tried in February 1677 at Paisley and all six 'condemned to the fire to be burned and their effigies with them'. Only Annabel, aged 14, was reprieved. Sir George's recovery was short. He died later the same year. The dumb girl recovered her speech and gave her name as 'Janet Douglas'. The story has been dramatised in a play by Anne Downie, *The Witches of Pollok.*

Sir George's son John succeeded and was created a baronet in 1682. He died childless and the title and lands passed to his cousin, John Maxwell of Blawarthill. This Sir John was a man of his time, the increasingly prosperous mid 18th century. He sent his son on the Grand Tour, began in 1747 to build Pollok House 'the small but genteel box', and interested himself in industry, granting a feu on his land at Pollokshaws for a printfield in return for a payment of £7 12s 5d sterling yearly, thus stimulating the growth of Pollokshaws as an industrial village. John's son, Sir Walter, carried on the old traditions however, with rents paid partly in services. A feu granted in 1761 to David Govan, weaver in Pollokshaws, required him to furnish 'a sufficient shearer one day in harvest

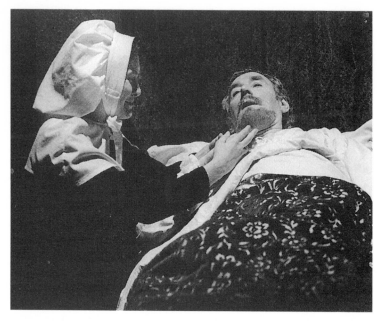

Hilary Maclean as the dumb girl and John Shedden as the bewitched Sir George Maxwell, in the Tron Theatre Company's production of The Witches of Pollok *by Anne Downie in 1990.*

yearly for each steading of dwelling house built, or to be built, on the said land or 10s Scots for each shearer'. In addition the said David was bound to grind his corn at the mill of Pollokshaws and to compear at the Courts of the Barony of Nether Pollok when called upon.

It was Sir John Maxwell, the 7th Bart, grandson of the builder of Pollok House, who carried out the clearance of Polloktoun in 1798.

Polloktoun is known from the 16th century and housed servants on the estate. On an estate plan of 1741 by Ogilvie, 'Pollok Town' is shown with several streets and 36 houses. The little village stood on the left bank of the Cart directly opposite the Laigh Castle, scanty remains of which are embedded in the garden wall beside the present Stable Courtyard. The workforce was resettled at Bogle's Bridge where they most likely found employment in the newly opened cotton mill. The reason given for the removal was the construction of the new road from Pollokshaws to the Hurlet

Pollock, the seat of Sir John Maxwell Bart, *from a print by Denholm, 1798.
The house was described as 'a small but genteel box'. Note the entrance
facing the river White Cart.*

via Cowglen, and the decision of Sir John to make the road the
southern boundary of his policies. By the end of the 18th century
the family had acquired almost all the land between the White
Cart and the Levern from Overlee in the east to Nitshill in the west
and as far north as the Clyde at Govan, along with lands on the
north of the Clyde. Sir John became the first Provost of the Burgh
of Pollokshaws in 1813.

By the time Sir John Maxwell, the 8th Bart, succeeded his father
in 1844, Pollokshaws had developed into a major centre for the
manufacturing and finishing of textiles. Many of the street names
associated with the family date from this period, although some
have now disappeared. Harriet, Matilda, Christian and Anne Streets
recall ladies of the family, Grantley a relative, Carment a family
solicitor, and Colledge the estate factor for whom the ruinous
Haggs Castle was restored as a house and office in the 1850s. Sir
John supported four schools within the Burgh, Pollok Academy,
an industrial school, a girls' school and a school for the children
of the miners at Titwood. When the Prince of Wales lunched at
Pollok House in 1859 after inspecting Mr Crum's calico-works at
Thornliebank, the school children, the estate workers, the Titwood
colliers and the Pollokshaws Brass Band all turned out to give his
Royal Highness a rousing welcome.

Sir John was succeeded by his nephew, Sir William Stirling-

Maxwell, son of his sister Elizabeth and Archibald Stirling of Keir. Sir William took little interest in the estate, spending his time at Keir or abroad, forming a collection of paintings, half of which came to Pollok when his son, Sir John Stirling-Maxwell, 10th bart, chose Pollok in preference to Keir when he came of age in 1888. Sir John extended the house and constructed the gardens. He hosted Scotland's first flying meeting in 1910 at Pollok when James Radley attained a height of 60 feet in a Bleriot monoplane. He had his architect Rowand Anderson alter Eastwood Parish Church and design a new Burgh Hall, liberally embellished with Maxwell coats of arms. Here in November 1912 the last Provost of Pollok-shaws demitted office and the Burgh was annexed to Glasgow.

Sir John's daughter, Mrs Anne Maxwell-Macdonald gifted the Pollok estate to the City of Glasgow in 1966 with provision for a site to house the Burrell Collection which was opened in 1983 adjacent to the former home farm, Knowehead.

Pollokshaws in the 18th century: a manufacturing yet rural village

The Rev Stevenson McGill, describing his parish of Eastwood in 1793, stated that the manufactures carried on were chiefly the weaving of muslins, bleaching, printing of calicoes, and cotton spinning. The Pollokshaws Society of Weavers dates from 1749 and handloom weaving was one of the earliest, and for more than a century, one of the principal employments in Pollokshaws. In 1782 the village contained 220 houses in which there were 311 hand-loom weavers employed by Paisley manufacturers in weaving fine silk gauze and linen. Possibly they also wove the fine quality linen cloth known as 'Bengals' which gave its name to Bengal Street. Despite the introduction of steam power for cotton weaving in the early 19th century, there still remained in Pollokshaws in 1836, several hundred handloom weavers working for the manufacturers of Glasgow and Paisley, but by the 1850s the industry was in decline. The last Pollokshaws weaver was James Harper who worked at his loom in a small shed near the Town Cross until his retirement in 1905.

Several early bleachfields were located along the Auldhouse Burn. One of these was near Auldburn Road, and another at Greenbank where later Thomas Baird, for many years Provost of the Burgh, built a dyeworks. The houses for his employees occupied the backlands behind Harriet Street and Baird's own mansion house stood on the site of the present children's playground in Greenbank Park. Newlandsfield Bleach Works were on an extensive site on the left bank of the Cart just north of the present Riverford Road. This ground was later occupied by a Glasgow Corporation Tram Depot and now by a supermarket.

In 1741 Archibald Ingram, attracted by the abundant waters of the Cart and especially its tributary, the Auldhouse Burn, feued land from Sir John Maxwell and formed a company 'for whitening and printing of calicos and linnens at Pollokshaws'. This was the first printfield in the west of Scotland. His partners were his brother-in-law John Glassford and other leading Glasgow merchants, eager to invest part of their fortunes made in the American and West India trade in this new venture into the textile finishing business. The chosen site lay close to the Auldhouse Burn on ground long after known as the Printfield Lands. This is now Auldhouse Retail Park, entered from Nether Auldhouse Road. To improve the water supply the original course of the burn was transformed into a mill lade and the burn itself diverted eastwards to its present course through Auldhouse Park.

Shortly after the dissolution of the Pollokshaws Printfield Company in 1789, John Monteith of Anderston erected the first large cotton spinning mill in the village on the site. In 1801 Monteith installed 200 power looms, making the mill the first commercially successful power-weaving establishment in Britain. The mill was lighted by the combustion of coal gas, another coup for Pollokshaws. Each of the 420 lights produced the light of three candles and afforded 'a brilliant and pleasing light to the numerous workers in that large factory...though sometimes an offensive smell arises from the escape of unconsumed gas'. This mill was later owned by J & R Cogan and renamed the Auldfield Weaving Factory.

The second large cotton mill in the district was at Thornliebank, now just outside the Glasgow City boundary. This business began as a printfield in 1778 and was taken over and expanded in 1789 by Alexander and James Crum. Robertson wrote of this mill in 1818:

> Here Messrs Alexander and James Crum, by their own well directed exertions, with the aid of machinery, have established a muslin or other cotton manufactory in all its branches, including printing, which

now gives bread to 1200 or 1500 people, where, 30 years ago, 3 families did not exist.

Thornliebank mill remained with the Crum family until taken over by the Calico Printers' Association in 1899 and finally closed in 1929.

Another very early industry in Pollokshaws was the shamy mill for the dressing, preparing and finishing of sheep and lamb skins in a process originally used to produce a fine, soft leather from the skins of the Alpine chamois. The mill was situated on the right bank of the Cart at the Shaw Bridge, just below the weir, and was started by the Tassie family, three of whom are described as skinners and one as a glover in the Poll Tax Roll in 1695. The best known member of the family is James Tassie, born in the village in 1735. Tassie studied at the Foulis Academy in Glasgow before leaving for Dublin to work in the jewellery trade. His reproductions of antique gems secured him international fame and the attention of Catherine the Great who paid over £2,000 for an order from Tassie. Tassie is best known today for his portrait medallions, some of which can be seen in the People's Palace.

A later owner, James Muirhead, made glue at the mill. This was firmly believed by the folk of the Shaws to give protection against cholera and other diseases. Children with Whooping cough were held over pots of glue by their mothers while the glue was being stirred. Glue-making was discontinued after Sir John Maxwell personally inspected the works in 1853 following complaints of the nuisance 'from the boiling of blubber and other noxious substances' by the residents of the Skin Mill Yard.

In the closing years of the 18th century the minister concluded that his parish seemed well adapted to manufactures and expressed a quiet satisfaction with the growing village of Pollok-shaws, situated in its fine valley and which 'affords from the surrounding eminence, a delightful prospect of a manufacturing yet rural village'. Some leading folk of the Shaws, however, realising that the rural village was poised on the brink of changes and alarmed by the dramatic increase in population, set up the Community of Pollokshaws. This was a form of local authority which, though possessed of few legal powers, exercised a very wide control from 1793 until 1813 when the village was erected into a Burgh of Barony with an elected Town Council.

The Community and the Burgh: few small communities are so famous as Pollokshaws

The Community, or Common Council of the Town of Pollokshaws, formed in 1793, was composed of all persons of good character, whether resident in the town or not, who paid the stipulated admission fees. The duties of the President, Treasurer and Councillors of the town, who served without salary of gratuity, were to acquire property and revenue and then use the income for the general good of the town, establishing schools, making new and repairing old wells, keeping up fire engines and lighting the streets and passages. One of the first acts of the officers was to obtain from Sir John Maxwell a legal title to the Common Muir, where the townsfolk's cattle were grazed. This was a two to three acre piece of ground on the west side of what is now Haggs Road. Adjoining the muir was a piece of uncultivated ground set aside for the 'Good Man', a perverted name for the 'Evil One', for the folk of the Shaws believed in the ancient custom of setting aside the 'Good Man's Croft', a piece of land for the use of the Devil and his followers who held their revels there. The 'Guid Man's Road' and the 'Guid Man's Bridge' are marked on old maps of the estate.

The ambition of the Community was to possess a Council Hall of their own, but the undertaking ultimately forced them into debt and dissolution. Fortunately part of the Town House survived the 1960s redevelopment of Pollokshaws village centre. A stone with the date 1803 can still be seen on the front wall of the only remaining part of the building, the steeple, or 'Clock Tower' as it is locally known.

The Community was also troubled by growing threats to law and order after clashes between local weavers and Irish navvies working on the Glasgow to Paisley canal. Work began on the canal in 1807 and by the summer of 1810 it had reached the vicinity of Pollokshaws. The labourers on the canal were lodged nearby at Dumbreck. The feud came to a head on 24 July with a clash between some of the townsfolk and a dozen or so navvies, when blows were exchanged and stones thrown. As a result two brothers, James and Charles Gallaugher, found themselves in court in Paisley accused of mobbing and assault. James admitted that he was present in Pollokshaws drinking and dancing, but did not remember the evening's events as he was very drunk and had gone to bed. Charles maintained that he had only gone to rescue his brother but had been set upon by the Pollokshaws mob who had started the whole affair. The outcome was sentences for Charles and James of six and twelve months respectively in Paisley Tolbooth.

At a meeting in November 1810 it was decided to apply for the town to be erected into a Burgh of Barony, and a charter was sealed at Edinburgh on 2 April 1813. The Burgh comprehended the town of Pollokshaws, along with Northhill, Shawhill, Coustonhill, Pollokshaws Printfield lands, Auldhousebridge and Catcraigs, with the right to a weekly market and two annual fairs on the first Tuesday of May and November for two successive days each. Sir John Maxwell was elected first Provost. The Bailie was James Drew surgeon, and the Treasurer David Patrick. The Councillors were James Wilson cooper, Robert Lang, John Campbell merchant, John Steel mason, Andrew Eadie baker, and James Young timber merchant.

In 1858 the Town Council adopted certain clauses of the Police Act of the preceding year and in 1892 became a Police Burgh in the full sense of the term. This enabled the Burgh to obtain a seal and a chain of office which was worn for the first time by Provost David Leckie at Queen Victoria's Diamond Jubilee celebrations at Buckingham Palace. A new Burgh Hall gifted by Sir John Stirling-Maxwell was opened in December 1898 and the centenary of the Burgh was celebrated by a dinner there attended by 130 gentlemen in October 1912. A few weeks later Robert Stirling Brown, the last Provost of Pollokshaws, demitted office and the Burgh was annexed to Glasgow on 5 November 1912.

Manufactures other than textiles were gradually introduced into Pollokshaws throughout the 19th century. The first forge was set up in 1830 in the Skin Mill Yard by James Muirhead who specialised in forging axles for railway engines. In 1848 he moved to larger premises at Crossmyloof, but retained the name Cart Forge. The first engineering firm was founded by William Stewart and Michael MacKenzie in Factory Street in 1857 making textile machinery. Cogan Street became a centre of engineering and contained more factories than any other part of the Burgh.

One of the most interesting local firms was the Victoria Pottery founded in Cogan Street in 1855 by Lockhart & Arthur, later David

The only remaining part of the Town Hall built by the Community of Pollokshaws is the Clock Tower. The date 1803 appears on the building.

Lockhart and Sons. For commercial reasons the products were stamped 'Made in Ireland'. The firm survived until 1952, longer than most other Glasgow potteries. Several items of pottery were displayed in Provand's Lordship in 1990, gifted by Sheila H Wylde, great grand-daughter of David Lockhart, in memory of her only son, killed in the Second World War.

Pollokshaws churches: they were men and women of rugged and sterling qualities of head and heart.

An almost straight line of churches starts at the Catholic church of St Mary Immaculate on Shawhill; continues south past the old Kirkyard and the Salvation Army Citadel in Bengal Street; past

173

Pollokshaws West United Free Church and Pollokshaws Parish Church in Shawbridge Street to the Methodist Church at the Round Toll; Eastwood Parish Church on the hill at Mansewood (built in 1862, replacing a church of 1781); and ends at the site of the old 17th-century Eastwood Parish Church and churchyard about a mile further south, now just within the Glasgow City boundary.

In 1764 a group of Seceders, who had formed a small praying society in Eastwood parish, were given permission to build a church in Kirk Lane. This was the earliest church in Pollokshaws. Fragments of two walls survive inside the kirkyard which was laid out round the church six years later. This congregation, known as the Associate Session of Pollokshaws, was split by a dispute in 1799 about how much power should be given to civil authorities. The larger group, known as the 'Auld Lichts' stoutly defended the Kirk's right to manage its own affairs without interference. This congregation continued to occupy the Old Kirk, then joined the Free Church and built a new church in Rossendale Road in 1870. This was in turn sold and demolished after a further union with Auldfield Church in 1929. Within the old burial ground in Kirk Lane, in the shadow of two multi-storey blocks and under the tumbled headstones, lie the daughter, two grandsons, a grand-daughter and the nephew of Robert Burns, Scotland's national poet — flow gently, sweet Cart, disturb not their dreams.

The 'New Lichts', the losers in the 1799 dispute, found new premises in an old drying kiln at Shaw Mill and became known as the 'Kiln Folk'. They built a church in 1814, known as the 'Five Cornered Kirk' because an adjoining proprietor refused to sell even a few yards of ground to square the site. The first minister was David Walker, of whom it was written, 'Troubles of exceptional quality clouded his closing years, when a female, subject to fits of derangement, who had been in his service, made accusations against his moral character'. In 1847 the 'Five Cornered Kirk' burned down after a fire was left burning in a new furnace 'to test how the flues, which were under the floor, would draw'. However, with the help of insurance money, 'a substantial erection rose without loss of time on the same site'. This was the church on the corner of Pollokshaws Road and Matilda Street which later became Pollokshaws Pollok Church of Scotland. The congregation was dissolved in 1976 and the property demolished.

A second group broke away from the Associate Session in

The church of St Mary Immaculate was built on Shawhill in 1864. The war memorial bears the names of men of St Mary's parish who died in the First World War.

protest against the choice of a minister, and in 1847 built their own church in Wodrow Street. This was the first United Original Secession Church in Glasgow and is now the parish church at 233 Shawbridge Street. The church originally had a dwelling for the minister on the upper floor, and in the time of the first minister, the Rev James Milne Smith, the manse was haunted by 'a harmless but boisterous ghost' in the spare bedroom. After ministering for 22 years in the Shaws, Mr Smith emigrated to New Zealand accompanied by a goodly number of his people, 'men and women of rugged and sterling qualities of head and heart', who formed a small colony in Auckland called Pollok Settlement. His successor

175

Sir John Maxwell School began as an industrial school in 1854. The present building was erected in 1909 and is now a primary school with a Gaelic Unit.

replaced the manse by a gallery and enjoyed a long, prosperous and undisturbed ministry. In 1956 the United Original Secession Church acceded to the Church of Scotland and the Pollokshaws church took the name Shawholm. It then united with Auldfield Parish Church in 1965 to form Pollokshaws Parish Church. This is now the last United Original Secession Church building in use for worship within the Church of Scotland.

It was 1830 before the Established Church granted a Chapel of Ease in Pollokshaws. The name Auldfield Chapel was chosen because the building at 169 Shawbridge Street was funded and built on ground owned by Messrs Cogan, owners of the Auldfield Weaving Factory, the largest cotton mill in the village. Auldfield became the parish church when Pollokshaws was disjoined from Eastwood parish in 1862. The church was demolished after the union with Shawholm in 1965. The bell and four stained glass windows were presented to the People's Palace and were at one time fitted in the Winter Garden there. The bell used to be rung daily to announce the closing of the gardens. Since 1965 there have been three ministers of Pollokshaws Parish Church: Walter Currie,

Ronald Johnstone and the present minister, the Rev Andrew Black. The congregation who worship today in the church represent all shades of tradition and belief within the Church of Scotland over a period of nearly two and a half centuries.

A mission for Catholic families was started in Pollokshaws in 1820 and Father Joseph Galetti was appointed as first resident priest in 1849. Services were held in a school until Muirhead's smithy in the Skin Mill Yard was converted into a chapel. The present church of St Mary Immaculate was built on the fine site on Shawhill in 1864 and the presbytery added some time later. The great-grandparents of Cardinal Thomas Winning were married in St Mary's and lived in Pollokshaws for the rest of their lives. The handsome war memorial in front of the church bears the names of the men of St Mary's parish who lost their lives during the First World War. A small school stood just to the west of the church until St Conval's Primary School on the top of Shawhill was built by the Eastwood School Board in 1906 with places for 960 boys and girls. St Conval is the patron saint of Eastwood parish.

The Parish School, Pollok Academy and Sir John Maxwell School

Until the 18th century Pollokshaws children attended the parish school at Eastwood which stood opposite the old church and churchyard on a site now occupied by Eastwood New Cemetery. An inquiry held in 1756 found that the greater part of the population of the parish lived in Pollokshaws, Bogle's Bridge and Auldhouse, and so a new parish school was built at Bogle's Bridge. This school served the parish for 34 years until a larger school was built at Cartcraigs in 1790. This was a two storey building with the school on the ground floor and the teacher's house above. On Richardson's map of 1795 the school is marked 'Eastwood Boarding Establishment' with the name of Mr Loudoun the parish schoolmaster underneath. The boarders appear to have included the sons of West Indian and Jamaican traders. Catcraigs was the area around the Round Toll and seems to have changed its name to Cartcraigs around this time.

In 1856 Sir John Maxwell built a new parish school at the corner of Pollokshaws Road and Matilda Street to a design by Alexander Thomson. The school was named Pollok Academy and bore a splendid Latin inscription on the west gable:

ACADEMIA PAROCHIALIS DE POLOC CULTURAE CHRISTIANAE
DEDICATA ANNO SALUTIS MDCCCLVI

After 1871 the Academy was managed by Eastwood School
Board. William Sewell served the Pollokshaws community from
1854 to 1891 first as parish schoolmaster, then as a distinguished
headmaster, receiving an LLD from the University of Glasgow and
becoming President of the EIS. In 1893 Pollok Academy was
recognised as a Secondary School, one of the earliest in Scotland.
The Secondary Department was later moved to Shawlands Academy and the Pollok building was unfortunately demolished in the
1960s.

By the middle of the 19th century a variety of day and evening
schools were operating in the Burgh, providing an elementary
education in the three R's. Some of these were attached to factories
such as Cogan's cotton mill. An industrial school was founded in
1854 on a site in Bengal Street gifted by Sir John Maxwell. The
boys chose a trade on entering, joiner, shoemaker or tailor, and
the girls were taught household skills. Both boys and girls could
grow produce for sale in one of the school's 40 plots. In 1872
Eastwood School Board took over the school and renamed it the
Sir John Maxwell School. It was replaced by the present red
sandstone building in 1909 and is now the local primary school.
In recent years one stream of pupils, at present one hundred of
the total roll of around 280, has formed the Gaelic Unit. The Gaels
spend two years learning Gaelic, then are bilingual and all their
classes are conducted in Gaelic. There is one head teacher for the
whole school.

John Maclean: we can make Glasgow a Petrograd, a revolutionary storm centre second to none

John Maclean was born on 24 August 1879 in Pollokshaws at 59
King Street (now part of Shawbridge Street). His father, Daniel
Maclean, was a potter in the Victoria pottery and died eight years
later of silicosis, the 'potters' disease'. His mother, Annie McPhee,
belonged to Nitshill and had worked as a powerloom weaver.
Maclean later lived in a house beside the Round Toll and after his
marriage to Agnes Wood of Hawick, set up house at Langside. He
later moved to a terraced house in Auldhouse Road, where he died
on 30 November 1923. The memorial to John Maclean in the centre
of the square at Shawbridge Arcade was unveiled by his daughter,

*John Maclean exchanges handshakes with workers during the 1919 strike.
In 1983 a memorial to Maclean was unveiled in the centre of his native
Pollokshaws by his daughter, Nan Milton, on the 50th anniversary of her
father's death.*

Nan Milton, on the 50th anniversary of Maclean's death. The
inscription reads:

> In memory of John Maclean.
> Famous pioneer of working class education,
> He forged the Scottish link in the
> Golden Chain of World Socialism.

It was at an open-air meeting beside the old Town House in
1906 that Maclean founded the Pollokshaws branch of the Social
Democratic Federation which had accepted Marxism in 1883. In
1910 he became actively involved in a strike of mill-girls at the
large thread mills at Neilston. Many of the girls belonged to Nitshill
mining families and with the assistance of the Federation of
Women Workers, Maclean was called on to organise the girls in a
campaign for better wages. The high point of the strike was when
the mill-girls marched down from Neilston to Pollokshields to
interview the manager at his residence there. The march, with a
great banging of tin cans and shouting and singing wended its
way through all the intervening villages to Pollokshields 'where

the respectable inhabitants were thoroughly disturbed'. A meeting was held in a field adjacent to the manager's house. The wage demands were met.

Of particular importance were the weekly evening classes which John Maclean gave at the Sir John Maxwell school from 1908–15, attended by huge audiences, including members of the Clyde Workers' Committee who became the leaders of the Red Clydeside movement during the First World War. Maclean had a MA degree from Glasgow University including political economy, His aim was to school the masses of workers on the basic principles of Marxism and eventually to establish a Scottish Labour College. The main text-book was *Das Kapital* and the courses were paid for by the Eastwood School Board of which Sir John was a leading member. Maclean also taught in several Glasgow schools, including Strathbungo, from which he was transferred after refusing to teach religious education, and Lorne Street, where his employment was terminated in 1915 by the Govan Parish School Board on the same day as he was sentenced for a breach of the Defence of the Realm Act.

A John Maclean Society was founded in 1968 and in 1973 two biographies were issued along with Homage to John Maclean, a collection of 31 songs from authors including Hugh MacDiarmid, Edwin Morgan and Matt McGinn who contributed *The Ballad of John Maclean*. These writings detail the important landmarks in Maclean's life: five prison sentences between 1915–22 for his revolutionary socialist and pacifist activities; the triumphal procession through the streets of Glasgow on his release from Peterhead after serving seven months of a five year sentence; his appointment as Russian Consul in January 1918; and Maclean's funeral when 10,000 people followed in procession to Eastwood Cemetery.

Ken Currie has painted John Maclean in one of his murals in the dome of the People's Palace and entitled it *Britain's leading Marxist intellectual at that time and above all a visionary*. Included in the picture is Maclean's one-time evening school assistant, James Maxton. Maxton was born in Pollokshaws in 1885 and became chairman of the ILP and MP for Bridgeton from 1922–46. He is honoured, not by a monument in his native village, but by a plaque in St James's School in the Calton, where he taught for ten years. Maxton's father taught at Pollok Academy and became headmaster of Grahamstone School in Barrhead.

Leisure activities in the Shaws

Until the end of the 18th century the main highway from Glasgow to Irvine led down the Shawhill, along Shawbridge Street, then up the Green Knowe towards Kennishead. The road crossed the Cart in the middle of the village by the old Shaw Bridge, built in 1654 and replaced by the present iron bridge in 1934. The part of Shawbridge Street north of the Cart was called Main Street and the part south of the river was King Street. In 1797 two new roads, Pollokshaws Road and Barrhead Road, were formed to avoid the steep hills to the north and south of Pollokshaws and to bypass the congested village centre. These roads joined up at the Round Toll, which became a regular stopping place for the Royal Sovereign stage coach from Irvine and the Levern Trader from Barrhead. The old toll-house dates from around 1800 and was extensively restored in 1995. It now stands in the middle of a modern roundabout. The house is circular with a conical roof and had a chimney stack in the centre. It is one of the few surviving local landmarks and one of the few toll-houses left in the Glasgow area.

At one time the Round Toll had a licence and was much frequented by racegoers at the Shaws Races which were held on Bangor's Hill, now part of Cowglen Golf Course. The 14th hole (196 yards, par 3) is named 'Race Course'. The race course was formed around 1839 by Sir John Maxwell, but races were held as far back as 1754 when the *Glasgow Mercury* announced that Pollokshaws Races would be held on Thursday 14 November. The horses, it was said, were certainly not equal to what one sees at Epsom or Doncaster, but the food on offer was unsurpassed, with the refreshment tents selling such delicacies as potted head and sheepshanks. The fame of the meeting was spread by the popularity of a ballad entitled *The Queer Folk i' the Shaws*, in which a Glasgow mother warns her simple-minded son of the hazards of a day at the Shaws Races.

Said she, 'Ye may be trod to death
Beneath the horses' paws;
An' mind ye, lad, the sayin's true —
There's queer folk i' the Shaws.'

The folks are green, it's oft been said,
Of that you'll find no trace;
There's seasoned wood in every head
And brass in every face.

Look smart and keep your eyes about,
Their tricks will make you grin.
The Barrhead bus will take you out,
The folks will take you in.

In the *Vagabond Songs of Scotland*, a version of the song is attributed to James Fisher, a native of Glasgow who was employed as a foreman in the Fereneze calico printworks at Barrhead. The song was a favourite with Jamie Blue, a street singer well known in the Shaws.

In 1896 the folk of the Shaws had the chance of a flutter in the State of Hamburg lottery, courtesy of an advert in the *Pollokshaws News*. Orders were to be addressed to Samuel Heckscher, Banker at Hamburg, with a cheque or postal order for six shillings for a whole ticket (half and quarter tickets also available). Total prize money 10 million 746,990 marks; the jackpot an amazing 500,000 marks.

In September the same year Sanger's world renowned Circus and Hippodrome came to Pollokshaws town. Top among the attractions were the Clairvoyant Talking Horse which would foretell the winner for every race through the year 1896; a parade of ostrich birds in cages; and Inecta Masunah, the Hottentot Venus, more powerful than any three ordinary men. Among the outdoor sports on offer, cycling was very popular, with a wide range of machines and accessories advertised: Raleighs, Triumphs, New Rapids, Flying Wheels and Stars from £8 10s to £25, all with pneumatic tyres and 'cyclealities' such as lamps, bells, inflators etc. Gentlemen could play golf at Cowglen or Pollok Golf Clubs, or cricket at the Poloc Cricket Club formed in 1878 and playing at a ground within the policies of the estate. Pollokshaws Bowling Club had a green on the east side of Pollokshaws Road from 1854 until the 1960s, since when the club has occupied a site on the west side of the road at Sheeppark.

Newlandsfield, beside Pollokshaws East railway station, is the ground of Pollok Football Club, a Junior football team which includes ex-professionals among its players. The team at present play in the Raebok Central League, attracting attendances of up to one thousand. In 1994 Pollok were champions in the Premier Division of the Junior Football League. At the south end of Auldhouse Road the Army Cadet Force (D Platoon RHF) and the Air Training Corps (2452 Shawlands Squadron) meet in a drill hall built

The Round Toll is one of the few surviving tollhouses in the Glasgow area, and now stands in the centre of a busy roundabout. The white building behind is Pollokshaws Methodist Church.

at the start of the century to look like a baronial castle. The public bowling greens, tennis courts and putting green in Auldhouse Park no longer exist, but facilities for indoor sports are now provided at Pollokshaws Sports Centre in the former public baths and washhouse building near the Shawbridge Arcade. These include a swimming pool, Turkish suite, sub aqua, a creche, keep fit and martial arts.

A piecemeal 19th century village, ripe for development

A survey carried out in 1957 by the City Architect and Planning Officer found the Pollokshaws area 'ripe for development'. Comprehensive development was judged the only practical remedy because of the bad layout and piecemeal 19th century development of the village and because of the extensive dilapidated property and substandard housing.

The survey found that of the 2,000 families in the area, 77%

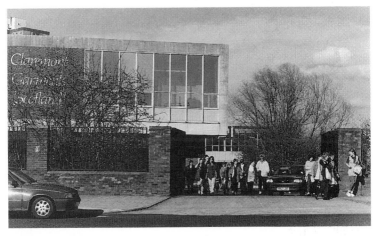

Textiles is an old established industry in Pollokshaws. Claremont Garments are the last of a long line of manufacturers on this site in Pleasance Lane.

lived in houses of one or two apartments. Only 23% had internal WCs, only 11% had baths, and 83% of the buildings could not be brought up to an acceptable standard. Half of the 128 shops were food shops or tobacconists or confectioners. There were 2 banks, 3 surgeries, 4 schools, 9 churches, 10 pubs, a post office and a cinema. The largest employer, with a workforce of 200, was James McFarlane & Co, shirt manufacturers in Pleasance Lane. Other firms with around 60–80 employees included John Dalglish & Sons textile machinery manufacturers, Compressor Services Ltd, and John McDonald & Co pneumatic tools. The Corporation Cleansing Depot at 135 Shawbridge Street had 44 employees. Three 'unsuitable processes' were identified: a scrap metal store, a rag sorting business and fish curing in Pleasance Lane.

The comprehensive development took place in the 1960s. In order to rehouse all the families living in the area (except households of six persons or over), about half the dwellings were in multi-storey blocks, the remainder in two, three or four storey developments. Industry was allocated six acres, public open spaces seven acres, and the shops were centred round the Shawbridge Arcade beside the Clock Tower.

A few tenements escaped obliteration, such as the building opposite the Clock Tower in Greenview Street. This contains the

Old Stag Inn, shown on the Ordnance Survey map of 1859. Another survivor was the line of red sandstone tenements on either side of the Old Swan Inn, at the corner of Pollokshaws and Haggs Roads. Ironically these were the first Glasgow tenements to be refurbished after the Council changed its policy from demolition to conservation in 1971, three years before the last of the Pollokshaws multi-storey blocks was completed. The letters JHG carved on the Old Swan Inn represent one of the Gilmour family, owners around 1901, the date carved on the building.

Despite wholesale redevelopment, Pollokshaws has succeeded in keeping its distinctive atmosphere, and the folk of the Shaws their own remarkable character. There is green parkland on three sides of the village, through which flow the clear waters of the Cart and the Auldhouse Burn, no longer known as the 'Red Dye Burn'. Clothing is manufactured by Claremont Garments in a modern factory for a leading British High Street store. The remaining landmarks, the Clock Tower, Burgh Hall, Sir John Maxwell School, Parish Church, Round Toll and Auldhouse, are the visible reminders of a community remarkable for its inventiveness, stubbornness, eccentricity, a people holding strong and extreme opinions, intractable, superstitious, ingenious and ingenuous, the Queer Folk of the Shaws.

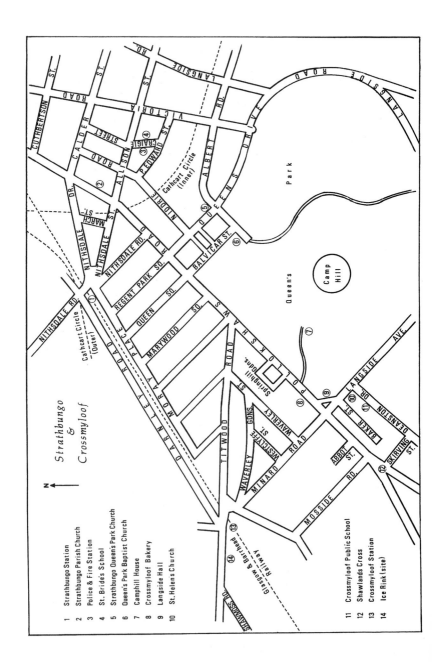

Strathbungo & Crossmyloof

N ←

1 Strathbungo Station
2 Strathbungo Parish Church
3 Police & Fire Station
4 St. Bride's School
5 Strathbungo Queen's Park Church
6 Queen's Park Baptist Church
7 Camphill House
8 Crossmyloof Bakery
9 Langside Hall
10 St. Helens Church

11 Crossmyloof Public School
12 Shawlands Cross
13 Crossmyloof Station
14 Ice Rink (site)

CHAPTER 9

STRATHBUNGO AND CROSSMYLOOF

Strathbungo and Crossmyloof grew up as small villages built along the Pollokshaws Road, one of the main arteries leading southwards from the centre of the city. Strathbungo is reached some two miles from Glasgow and Crossmyloof lies a mile further on. The villages were separated by the Camphill estate, now part of the Queen's Park. Neither village ever achieved burgh status, and both were annexed to Glasgow in 1891.

Strathbungo lay just inside Govan parish on its boundary with Cathcart parish and at one time the line of Allison Street and Nithsdale Street formed the boundary or 'march' between the counties of Lanark and Renfrew. The old name for Strathbungo was 'Marchtown' and this survives in March Street. The words 'Strathbungo Cross' appear on a tenement at the corner of Allison Street and Pollokshaws Road, but no satisfactory explanation has ever been given for the name 'Strathbungo'.

The old name for Crossmyloof was Westfield, and the village occupied a wedge of land on the western extremity of Cathcart parish. It has been suggested that the curious name Crossmyloof comes from the Gaelic *Crois Moaldhuibh*, the Cross of Malduff, an early Celtic saint. Some kind of cross dedicated to the saint may well have marked the western boundaries of the ancient parish of Cathcart at the point where it met Eastwood and Govan. The boundary between Cathcart and Eastwood passed just north of Skirving Street and along Mossside Road, where it also met Govan parish. The name Crossmyloof Mansions can be seen on the gushet building at Shawlands Cross, while the name Shawlands Cross appears on a tenement at the corner of Skirving Street and Kilmarnock Road.

Traditional associations of the name Crossmyloof with Mary Queen of Scots nevertheless die hard, and nowhere more so than above the doors of the Corona Bar, situated at the corner of Langside Avenue and Pollokshaws Road, where there are replicas of an open hand, representing the Queen's palm or 'loof', holding the ebony cross on which she is supposed to have solemnly sworn to meet the Regent in battle that fateful day.

Popular tradition connects the name of Crossmyloof with the Battle of Langside. Above the doors of the Corona Bar, the replica of an open hand represents Queen Mary's palm or 'loof' holding a cross on which she is supposed to have sworn to meet the Regent in battle.

Strathbungo village: crofters, colliers, weavers and carters

Strathbungo developed as a crofters' and miners' village after Sir John Maxwell of Nether Pollok began to feu out the lands of Titwood in the early 18th century. On a plan of 'Marchtown' drawn in 1741 by Robert Ogilvie, a local surveyor, the village is divided into four quarters by the intersection of Pollokshaws Road with a highway running from east to west, represented today by the line of Allison Street and Nithsdale Street. The north-west and south-west quarters are named as North Cammeron and South Cammeron. The names of some of the early feuars are known from feu charters granted by Sir John. In 1727 Andrew Shiells, maltman, son of John Shiells in Titwood, was given a feu of land in North Cammeron, and an adjacent feu was later acquired by William Neilson, a thatcher. In 1741 the map shows a continuous line of

The Strathbungo Public School Maypole Dance Team who competed in the Queen's Park in June 1900.

buildings along the Pollokshaws Road at North Cammeron. The area behind the buildings is marked 'Cameronseye' and probably contained the kind of small, slanting coal workings known as an 'ingaun ee' ('ingoing eye') which could be worked from the surface by a collier.

In the north-east quarter of the village, an early feu was granted to Houston of Jordanhill and Dunlop of Garnkirk. These men may have been working the upper seams of the Govan colliery in the Strathbungo area. This ground was sold in 1790 to a shoemaker called John Wallace. The south-east portion of the village is named on Ogilvie's map as the Spittle Croft, suggesting a possible connection with Hutchesons' Hospital. David Muir, a collier, was given a feu here in 1773. The names of David Neilston, a weaver, and his neighbour, David Ross, a collier, appear in another feu granted in 1800. Ross is said to have had an old pit in his garden and to have wheeled the coal from it in a barrow to the mouth of the close and sold it there. At the end of the 18th century 35 families were living in the village, and weaving had now become the principal occupation. The introduction of weaving to Strathbungo is credited to John Houston, a weaver from Paisley. His son, William, who set up as a manufacturer, at one time had 80 weavers in the village working for him.

The four quarters of Strathbungo were gradually built over by 'lands'. These were normally two-storey buildings erected by tradesmen to house themselves and their employees: Storie's Land by a cartwright; Little's Land by a cabinet maker; Smith's Land by a grocer; Nelson's Land by a gardener. Other 'lands' in the village in the middle of the 19th century were Edminston's, Graham's, Tosh's, Wallace's, Curr's, McDougall's and Campbell's. By the 1850s there were a few Irish families from Fermanagh, County Tyrone and Donegal, mostly housed in Boyd's Row. Some families from Argyll were also scattered through the village. By now the colliers had all left Strathbungo, and the range of occupations had widened to include several carters, blacksmiths, a railway porter and a pianoforte maker. These lands gradually disappeared when tenement building started around the 1870s.

Churches and Schools

Strathbungo had no church of its own until a Chapel of Ease was erected in 1838, five years after a mission was begun in the village. A church was built two years later and in 1848 the Rev Alexander Sutherland was appointed as the first minister. This church, situated in a side street on the east side of Pollokshaws Road in the north part of the village, became the parish church of Strathbungo when the parish was disjoined from Govan in 1879. Seven years later a new church was built on the east side of Pollokshaws Road just north of Allison Street. This building, with its distinctive lantern tower, was vacated after the congregation were united with Queen's Park West Church of Scotland in 1979, and was sold to the Pakistani community for use as educational premises. The Rev Norma Stewart has been minister of the united congregation of Strathbungo Queen's Park since 1979.

Queen's Park West Church began in 1867 as a Free Church congregation and met in a small hall until the present church in Queen's Drive was built in 1874 to a design by James Thomson. The *Centenary History* of the church contains an interesting account of the life and work of the church and the community it served. The first beadle, John Cameron, was dismissed when he 'breached his pledge of teetotalism'. D C Nicol, the congregational treasurer, made off to New York with the church funds, then wrote back and asked for his 'lines' to be sent on. He was refused. Despite these set-backs the church was active in a full range of activities: Sunday Schools, YMCA, Literary Society, Boys' Brigade,

One of the South Side's finest churches, the former Camphill Queen's Park Church of Scotland, designed by William Leiper. The building was recently restored and is now Queen's Park Baptist Church.

Dorcas Society, Musical Association and Womens' Foreign Missionary Society. The programme for the Band of Hope in 1910 included lectures entitled *Beware of the Dog, Dead Walls, St George and the Dragon,* and one delivered by the minister, the Rev J L Craig, on *Rambling about London.* In 1953 the Craig Chapel was dedicated in honour of Mr Craig, who had served the congregation for 60 years.

Two stained glass windows in the vestibule commemorate Jane Haining who died at Ausschwitz in July 1944. Jane Haining joined the congregation as a young woman, trained as a missionary and refused to leave her post as matron of a Jewish Girls' Home in Budapest after the outbreak of war in 1939. She was arrested and imprisoned without trial in May 1944 and died from starvation two months later, the only Scot to die in a Nazi concentration camp. Round the corner from the church in Niddrie Road is Langside Synagogue, built in 1926. The synagogue takes its name from Langside Road, where the congregation first met in 1914 in a former shop.

Although Strathbungo had no church of its own until 1838, a school in Strathbungo at the beginning of the 19th century enjoyed a reputation far beyond the village, and was attended by the children of local farmers and youngsters from Langside and Crossmyloof. The master was Mr Auld who became a minister in Greenock. The school was at first housed in a series of make-shift premises, but in 1840 the minister of Govan reported that a schoolhouse, with a dwelling house for the school-master attached, had been built by private subscription. This school was situated in March Street.

After the annexation of Strathbungo by Glasgow, Strathbungo Public School was built on the east side of Craigie Street and has the date 1894 on the building. The school opened with a roll of over 1,000 pupils and became a Higher Grade school with the addition of a Science Department in 1899 and a Commercial Department in 1900. The first headmaster was George Watson BA. The school quickly earned a reputation for its teaching of mathematics and foreign languages. For twenty years M Janton and Herr Dr Lubovius gave tuition as visiting teachers of French and German. The school is now St Bride's Primary School. At the north end of Strathbungo, Cuthbertson Primary School was opened in 1906 and in 1912 Hutchesons' Girls' Grammar School was built in Kingarth Street. This is now the Junior School.

Public service: the Police Force and the Third Lanarkshire Rifle Volunteer Corps

Following the annexation of Strathbungo by Glasgow in 1891, imposing new public buildings were built in the area between Allison Street and Prince Edward Street. This was the old Spittal Croft and from 1879 it had been occupied by Hutchesons' Gardens, which now moved to their final home at Crossmyloof. In 1896 a new police station and fire station were opened on the west side of Craigie Street, opposite the school. These replaced former police premises in March Street. Except for a small police office, the police station and fire station have both been converted into apartments. An area in front of Prince Edward Street has never been built over because of old coal workings underground and has been left as a car-park. On 30 December 1969 a tragic incident occurred when DC Angus Mackenzie was shot dead and two other officers from the station seriously injured when they were called to a ground floor flat in Allison Street to investigate a bank robbery carried out earlier the same day at a branch of the Clydesdale Bank at Linwood. One of the three armed robbers escaped, but was recaptured later the same night at Paisley.

Another public building still in use in Strathbungo is the former Third Lanarkshire Rifle Corps drill hall in Coplaw Street. This is now the premises of Brown's Health and Leisure Club. The building was formally opened as the head-quarters of the Company in May 1885. On the first floor, the large room with oriel windows was the officers' mess. The upper lights of the windows were originally filled with stained glass, as were those of the colonel's room on the first floor of the tower. As well as a drill hall and gymnasium, the building contained facilities for the numerous regimental activities. According to the *Third Lanark Chronicle*, in 1896 the dramatic club produced *Our Boys*, *The Area Belle* and *Cut Off with a Shilling*; the gymnastic club beat the redoubtable DAGS (Dundee Amateur Gymnastic Club) in the second round of the Scottish Associations Challenge Shield; the 26 members of the orchestral society met every Monday at 8pm for practice; the whist club were 'very unfortunate' having played 10 matches, lost 7, won 2, and tied 1.

Other regimental activities included competing at the National Rifle Meetings at Bisley, and summer parades and 'field days' at Pollok on the estate of Sir John Stirling-Maxwell, Hon Colonel of the Regiment. On one exciting exercise held in the grounds, a detachment of the Third Lanark were required to proceed to Pollok House, seize the bridge over the Cart and place Pollok House in a state of defence. Despite a navigational error by the motor cycle scouts, followed by a retreat to Sheep Park farm, the mission was satisfactorily accomplished.

The regiment was founded as part of the great Volunteer movement which began in 1859 when half the British army was abroad in India or the colonies. The official returns for 1884 gave an enrolled strength of 214,000 men of all ranks. After some dispute with companies formed in the West End and by the University, the 'Southrons' were designated the Third Lanarkshire Rifle Volunteer Corps. In the early years the uniform was dark grey with a cap, then scarlet with a shako, then scarlet with royal blue facings and a helmet. The figure of a Colour Sergeant wearing the uniform of 1878–91 is on display in the Kelvingrove Museum. The highlight of the year 1859 was when 380 men of the eight Lanarkshire Companies formed part of Queen Victoria's Guard of Honour at the opening of the Loch Katrine waterworks. This was the first time that citizen soldiers ever had the honour of appearing under arms before the Queen. The Volunteers travelled by train to Balloch, then boarded a steamer for the sail up Loch Lomond to Inversnaid. The rain was falling, not in soft and gentle showers, but in blinding sheets of cold and drenching water', and on the march to Loch Katrine the rain fell 'in blinding torrents'. The downpour eased only during the ceremony, when the Queen touched a lever which raised the sluices and sent pure water flowing down to Glasgow.

Jeems Kaye's Stra'bungo

The opening of Strathbungo Parish Church in 1886 coincided with the appearance in the *Bailie* of a series of letters written to the magazine by 'Jeems Kaye'. These letters gave a commentary on life in Strathbungo in particular and Glasgow in general and made the name of Strathbungo famous in the city. In a light-hearted manner they discuss the popular issues of the day through the mouths of the fictitious Sir Jeems Kaye, Bart, proprietor of the local coal ree, elder of the kirk, Lt Colonel of the 1st Royal Stra'bungo Fusiliers and Provost of the burgh of Stra'bungo, his wife Betty, his friends and associates.

In the letter which appeared in the *Bailie* in September 1887, Jeems explains how he is helping to raise funds for a new kirk:

> We - that is, the minister an' me between us - hae filled the kirk tae overflowin', and haein' had tae turn awa' dizzens o' applicants, we've nae alternative than tae erect a new ane, ane mair suited to the times than oor dear auld biggin' which was only meant for Stra'bungo when it wis a bit colliers' clachan. So we're tae hae a bazaur.

The bazaar will have a moving waxwork, better than McLeod's in the Trongate; an 'Art Gallery' whose rare and costly pictures will surpass anything seen at the exhibitions in Manchester or

A sketch from the Bailie *15 June 1887. Sir Jeems Kaye, the fictitious Provost of the Burgh of Stra'bungo, and Colonel of the 1st Royal Stra'bungo Fusiliers, rides at the head of his men. At his side Mr Pinkerton the Senior Bailie, who was run over by a tramcar, stumps along on his 'wudden leg'.*

Edinburgh; and a series of lectures, including Mrs McCracken the postmistress on 'The dark secrets o' the postal service, as gathered frae fifteen years' diligent reading o' the post cards' and Mr McCunn's paper on 'The ancient canoe an' the two Roman haufcroons found in the bed o' the river Bungo during the late dry summer'. The refreshment stand will not be licensed, but lime juice and milk and 'Zoedone' will all be available.

In an issue of the *Bailie* the following January, Jeems, his face washed, his court suit on, and lighting his cigar, is off in a cab to the courthouse in Glasgow to press his case to the Boundaries

Commission who are investigating Glasgow's threat to annexe the burgh of Stra'bungo, the burning issue of the time. 'Are you Strabungonians a happy and united community?' asks the chairman. 'Like a band o' brithers' replies Sir Jeems. 'We hae one kirk, one hall, one school, an' if one has sassages for his dinner the hale toon kens about it jist as if the bellman had cried it'. Sir Jeems wins his case and the chairman concludes that 'Whatever we do with Crosshill and Govanhill, and all these mushroom burghs - and its likely we will annexe them to Glasgow - Strathbungo must free'. 'Aye' agrees Jeems, 'free and unfettered'. The letters were later published in book form by the author, Archibald MacMillan, who lived in the village, and based his characters on real villagers.

As might be expected in a village at the junction of two important routes, Strathbungo had several noted hostelries. There was the Cross Keys almost opposite the church, and the Hunter's Inn on the east side of the Pollokshaws Road south of the village. Best known, however, was Granny McDougall's Inn, sometimes called the 'Robert Burns Tavern' which stood at the north-west corner of the junction and had a sign-board with a picture of the poet. Strathbungo even had its own Bonnie Jean.

> The Glasgow lasses gang fu' braw
> And country girls gang neat and clean,
> But nane o' them's a match awa
> To my sweet maid, Strathbungo Jean.

> Tho' they be dressed in rich attire,
> In silk brocade and mous-de-laine,
> Wi' busk and pad and satin stays,
> They'll never ding Strathbungo Jean.

Regent Park; Alexander Thomson's Southern Suburb

The development of Regent's Park as a residential suburb to the south-west of Strathbungo began in 1859 when nos 1–10 Moray Place were built to the design of Alexander Thomson. The remainder of Moray Place was built by speculative builders to more conventional designs. The other terraces, Regent Park Square, Queen Square and Marywood Square, formed a private estate, exclusive enough to have gates. The surviving pillars can be seen at the east end of Regent Park Square. This part of Strathbungo was designated a conservation area in 1973. These houses were occupied by merchants, manufacturers and professional men who could conveniently travel into the city by train from Strathbungo station which was opened in 1877 by the Glasgow, Barrhead and Kilmarnock Joint Railway. The station is now closed. The district was popular with government and other officials. These included John Fairservice, detective officer for the county of Renfrew, William Munro, surveyor of stamps, and Ralph Moore, government inspector of mines. The *Glasgow Post Office Directory* for 1870–71 lists eleven clergymen resident in the area, the incumbents of Kinning Park Free, East Campbell Street Free, Queen's Park Free, North Hanover Street Congregational and Laurieston Parish churches in Queen Square; Maitland Free, Langside Road United Presbyterian and Eglinton Street Congregational in Moray Place; Trinity Free and Stockwell Free in Regent Park Square; and Camphill United Presbyterian church in Regent Park Terrace.

Alexander Thomson's own house was no 1 Moray Place, and is now an A-listed building. The house was extended in the same style around 1930. Thomson had previously resided for most of his married life at Apsley Place in Laurieston, but after four of his children died of cholera between 1854 and 1857, he moved his family briefly to Darnley Terrace in Shawlands, and then settled permanently at Moray Place. Most of his work was done while living there. It is regrettable that so many of Thomson's outstanding buildings on the south side of the city have been lost. Fortunately two villas have survived in nearby Pollokshields: Ellisland at 200 Nithsdale Road, and the Knowe at 301 Albert Road, both in private ownership. The row of tenements at nos 84–112 Nithsdale Road were begun around 1873 and have the typical 'Greek' Thomson band over the upper windows. They may have been designed by William Turnbull, Thomson's partner, after Thomson's death in 1875.

In the 1890s Charles Rennie Mackintosh lived at 27 Regent Park Square. His father had been promoted to Superintendent of Police in 1889 and had remarried and moved the family home from Townhead to Strathbungo. This must have pleased Mackintosh, who as winner of the Alexander Thomson Scholarship had been able to spend the year 1891 in Italy. Charles had a room in the basement at Regent Park Square hung with Japanese and pre-Raphaelite prints. He was at this period working in the office of Honeyman and Keppie, and it was also at this time that he met his future wife, Margaret MacDonald and won the competition for the design of the Glasgow School of Art.

Crossmyloof village: vagrants, weavers and bloom worshippers

In 1818 Crossmyloof was described as the most populous Village in Cathcart parish. Although till recently 'remarkable chiefly for being a resort of vagrants', the writer was happy to report that the village had now become more respectable from an increase in the number of its inhabitants, who now amounted to around 500. The remarks were a little premature, because in November 1820 two members of a band of armed ruffians who robbed a house in Crossmyloof were hanged in front of the Jail in the Saltmarket. The attack took place at the home of Dr Robert Watt, the author of the four volume *Bibliothica Britanica*, who had died, allegedly of overwork, the previous year. His terrified widow had a pistol held at her head and her gold rings wrenched off her fingers. She is reported as having hastily left Crossmyloof for the safety of a home in Hutchesontown.

When the Rev James Smith wrote his account of Cathcart parish in 1840, he used the name Westfield for the village and gave the number of families as 124 and the total population as 587 persons. At this period the villagers were mostly cotton handloom weavers. The only remaining woollen weaver was William Algie, assisted by his seven children, three of whom wove woollen cloth, and four worked in cotton. Two elderly women, Mary Sinclair a muslin flowerer, and Margaret Wotherspoon a muslin tambourer, were probably the last of the skilled embroideresses in the village. There were also a few shop-keepers, a blacksmith, several brassfounders and tinsmiths and William Ferguson, a lithographic engraver. By 1851 the population had risen sharply to 939 persons. The rise was accounted for by the establishment of the Crossmyloof Bakery in 1847 by Neale Thomson of Camphill. The following year James Muirhead moved his Cart Forge from its original site in the Skin Mill Yard at Pollokshaws to larger premises at Crossmyloof, where he produced axles for railway waggons. The Cart Forge was situated between Baker Street, where Thomson's workforce was housed, and the Pollokshaws Road.

Although most of the villagers lived along the Pollokshaws Road, then known in the centre of the village as Cathcart Place, there was another small community in the area between Titwood Road and Mossside Road. (Minard Road was not formed until

Looking north from Shawlands Cross along Pollokshaws Road. This was the main street of Crossmyloof village, and was known as Cathcart Place. The Glasgow Savings Bank building (now TSB) was erected in 1906 .

around 1900). This area was known as Langside Valley and contained a few villas and cottages and several orchards and nurseries. This was where Glaswegians came in the summer to enjoy fresh air and healthy surroundings. An advertisement in the *Glasgow Courier* of 25 February 1802 offers two 'neat' lodgings at the village of Westfield for renting as summer quarters for 'genteel families' from the city, who would find the houses well adapted for their use with the convenience of good water and a 'neat' plot of ground. Applications to be made to David Erskine, gardener at Westfield. The villa owners included James Smellie, a retired cooper who occupied the house called Langside Valley, William Jaffrey, an accountant and notary public and owner of Campvale

House. Springhill House was the residence of Henry Murphy, a pawnbroker and hat manufacturer in the Bridgegate. The house later became Springhill Academy with William Cairns and William Christie as joint headmasters. Archibald McAuslan was the local surgeon and physician, and the community included a group of customs officers with the titles of outdoor officer, running officer, clerk, weigher and locker.

When Hugh MacDonald passed through Crossmyloof on one of his *Rambles* in 1851, he found that the weavers of Crossmyloof and Strathbungo, like their neighbours on the hill above at Langside, were 'celebrated growers of tulips, pansies, dahlias and other floricultural favourites' and met regularly at their florist clubs to examine choice flowers and discuss the best means of rearing them to perfection. Of these 'bloom worshippers' MacDonald writes:

> There are some sharp-sighted people who are said to see further into a millstone than their neighbours. For the truth of the saying we shall not venture to vouch; but most assuredly, for seeing into the mysteries of a tulip or a dahlia, we shall back a Crossmyloof or Strabungo weaver against the united amateurs of Scotland.

The Hutchesontown Gardens started in 1835 as allotments for the pastime of growing fruit, flowers and vegetables, moved to Govanhill, then to Strathbungo, and finally in 1892 to Crossmyloof Gardens off Shawmoss Road, and continued there until 1965 when they were built over for housing.

In his report on the parish, the minister also explained that a 'large and excellent school' under the patronage of Neale Thomson of Camphill, served the inhabitants of Crossmyloof and district, although it stood just across the boundary within Eastwood parish. The parish boundary was formed here by the Waterland stream, and its course can be traced between the ruinous remains of two old walls behind the school building on the north side of Skirving Street, now used as shops. Mr Smith describes how a number of years before, when there was no teacher for two years, the inhabitants, mostly weavers, formed themselves into an educational society to be managed by twelve directors under the presidency of the minister, and some of the 'more intelligent' of the villagers undertook the task of teachers:

> a room was hired for the purpose, and a school opened from 8 to 10 o'clock at night, in which the teachers, two by two, in monthly turn, gave gratuitous instruction to whatever children were committed to

their charge. The duty of the directors was principally to visit the school, and to wait upon careless parents to urge upon them the propriety of securing to their children the advantages which it offered.

In 1877 the Cathcart School Board built Crossmyloof Public School in Stevenson (now Deanston) Drive. This school building is being converted into twelve two-bedroom and four one-bedroom flats, to be known as Deanpark Court. The name of the school could be seen on the front of the building until conversion began, but this reminder of old Crossmyloof has now also disappeared.

The first church to be erected in Crossmyloof was Langside Road Church (later Langside Avenue). This was built in 1859 for a United Presbyterian congregation which had been formed two years previously. The site at the corner of Baker Street and Langside Avenue was gifted by Neale Thomson. A new church was built on the same site in 1896. The congregation united with that of Shawlands Old in 1963 and the Langside Avenue buildings became St Helen's Catholic Church.

Elizabeth Burns

For several years no. 3 Woodside Terrace, Crossmyloof, was the home of Elizabeth Burns, the daughter of the poet Robert Burns and Anna Park, the niece of Mrs Hyslop of the Globe Inn in Dumfries. The house was later renumbered as 1094 Pollokshaws Road. It stood near the corner of Abbot Street. The building is now demolished and the site is occupied by a Co-operative supermarket.

'Betty Burns' as the poet's daughter was commonly known, was born on 31 March 1791 in Leith, where her mother had gone to stay with a sister, in whose house Elizabeth remained for two years. She was then brought up and educated with the rest of Burns's children at Dumfries and cared for kindly by Jean Armour until at the age of 18 she married John Thomson and left Dumfries for good. Betty's daughter Margaret later told a friend that when her mother was married, Jean Armour 'sent her out as if she had been her own daughter'. John Thomson served in the army until 1814 and during that period his wife stayed at Pollokshaws with his family, spending her time doing needle flowering for a Glasgow warehouse. After leaving the army John Thomson worked as a weaver. The couple first lived in Langside village then moved back

Elizabeth Burns was the daughter of the poet and Anna Park of the Globe Inn in Dumfries. 'Betty' Burns married John Thomson, a Pollokshaws weaver, and lived at Langside, Pollokshaws and Crossmyloof.

to Pollokshaws where they brought up their family at no 10 Pollok Street (now Greenview Street). Jean Armour continued to take an interest in Betty, writing to her and enclosing small gifts for the children.

Betty Burns died at Woodside Terrace in 1873, four years after her husband, and is buried at the old Kirk Lane burial ground in Pollokshaws with other members of her family. Her elder son, Robert Burns Thomson, was a brush manufacturer and lived at Carment Drive in Shawlands. The younger son, James Glencairn Thomson, was unmarried and was a calico engraver. He lived in Crossmyloof until his death in 1911 and was a well known singer of his grandfather's songs and a frequent player on the green of the Camphill Bowling Club in the park at the foot of Langside Avenue. A gift of money raised by public subscription and a pension from the Civil List in recognition of the eminence of his grandfather, made his last years more comfortable.

The Crossmyloof Bakery: a monster baking manufactory

The Crossmyloof Bakery was begun by Neale Thomson of Camphill in 1847 to supply wholesome and reasonably priced bread for his own workforce, employed in his cotton mills in Hutchesontown. In response to an almost immediate wider demand, a shop was opened in Crown Street, where the arrival of the loaves was awaited by large crowds.

> The struggle was often extreme; shawls were torn off the shoulders of the women, and men emerged in a triumphant but disordered condition from the mass, waving in triumph the reward of their labours, and shouting, 'This is the poor man's loaf, my boys'.

The bakery was situated in Pollokshaws Road, across from Camphill House. Several buildings remain, now in use as a bedding factory and sales room, but are obscured from the main road by the large tenement building known as Camphill Gate.

The Crossmyloof Bakery rapidly became something of a visitor attraction on the south side of the city. It was visited by Hugh MacDonald in 1851, who called it 'probably the largest of the kind in the queen's dominions'. Mr Dalgetty, the manager, led the party on a tour and explained the various activities of the 45 to 60 bakers who attended the 26 ovens and transformed a weekly average of five hundred sacks of flour into around 40,000 quartern loaves. Other employees loaded up the six large vans which constantly carried the loaves to the various outlets in the insatiate city. MacDonald was forced to admit that cleanliness, order and neatness pervaded every department, and seldom had he seen a more curious or cheerful sight than these spacious bakehouses where:

> 30 well-powered operatives are busily engaged thumping, pelting, turning, cutting, weighing, and kneading immense masses of plastic dough, which, in their experienced hands, rapidly assumes the requisite form and consistency.

Accommodation for the skilled workforce was provided in the Baker Row, two long, grey rows of cottages which stood in Baker Street, off Langside Avenue. The sheltered housing erected by the Margaret Blackwood Housing Association now occupies the site. In 1851 the houses in the row were occupied by Joseph Dalgetty, the manager, eleven journeymen bakers and a journeyman brewer. The men were mostly from Edinburgh and the Lothians, married men in their late twenties and thirties. Dalgetty was a native of Ayton in Berwickshire.

At first Thomson was troubled by competitors who placed his loaves within three feet of a good fire for seven to eight hours to dry them out, then complained to an inspector that they were underweight. The ruse did not work, and during a protracted correspondence in the *Glasgow Courier* and the *Glasgow Herald*, Thomson confounded his opponents by proving scientifically that a four pound loaf did not contain four pounds of flour, as only the ignorant would expect.

After Neale Thomson's death in 1857, the cotton mill and the bakery were carried on by his widow and son. A downturn in the cotton trade forced the mill to close in 1880. Shortly after, the bakery closed in the face of stiff competition from 'Stevenson's Machine-Made Bread'. By 1888 J & B Stevenson were producing 100,000 loaves a day 'untouched by human hand' in their gigantic bakeries at Cranstonhill and Plantation.

The Crossmyloof Bakery premises were bought around 1890 by Lockhart Smith & Co, proprietors of Lockhart's Cocoa Rooms, who had previously traded at Bishop Street in Anderston. Lockhart's operated a chain of shops in Glasgow and in the Newcastle area, where the public could enjoy tea, coffee, cocoa, aerated drinks and 'eatables in great variety' at low prices in small, clean premises. The firm became Lockhart's Tea Rooms as tea replaced cocoa as the fashionable drink. In 1919 they had 13 branches in Glasgow, at Gordon, Renfield, Sauchiehall, Jamaica and High Streets, at Bridgeton Cross, Trongate, Candleriggs and Paisley Road Toll, and no less than four tearooms for weary and thirsty shoppers in Argyle Street. After the war, tastes again changed, and the tearooms became cafes, but Lockhart's finally succumbed to competition from Ross's Milk Bars as fashions again changed in the 1930s.

Marlborough House, at the foot of Langside Avenue, was built in 1915 by William Kerr, according to the *Bailie* 'one of the most enterprising caterers in the west'. Kerr was a chef who made his name in Glasgow by running a tearoom at the 1911 Exhibition. He then learned the techniques of mass catering during the war. The magazine noted that in equipment and general appearance 'this new restaurant will far outdistance anything yet dreamed of on the South Side'. Kerr was, however, infamous for the poor conditions he imposed on his staff. His waitresses were paid 12 shillings per week for a 12 hour day and fined two shillings if they broke a wineglass, and nine pence for a cup. The Marlborough was later bought over by A F Reid & Sons, who also bought over Kerr's premises in Victoria Road. Marlborough House was bought by Reo Stakis in 1968, but shortly after was gutted by fire and redeveloped, and is now a club.

The Camphill Estate

The estate of Camphill now forms part of the Queen's Park, and the name derives from a circle of stones and earthworks near the highest point of the park. The earthworks are thought to be of Iron Age date. Excavations have revealed part of an inner stockade, and medieval pottery has been recovered from the ditch and Roman sherds from the bank. The site has been interpreted variously and unconvincingly as a camp associated with Romans, or Caledonians, or Queen Mary, after whom the park is named.

According to Semple, continuing Crawfurd's *History of the Shire of Renfrew*, Mr Crawfurd of Posle built a good house on the south side of the great road betwixt the village of Pollokshaws and Glasgow in 1777 'adjacent to the bottom of the north side of Langside Hill, near to which is a small plantation of firs'. Richardson's map of 1795 shows a house beside trees at Camphill with the name of the owner, Thos Crawfurd. When Robertson once again updated Crawfurd's *History* in 1818, he reported that the owner of the handsome dwelling called Camphill was now Robert Thomson Esq. Camphill House is an elegant classical house containing a simple interior with a compact oval staircase. There has been much speculation about the date of building and the identity of the architect.

The Thomson family originated in Tulliallan, and were owners of the Adelphi Cotton Works in Hutchesontown. Robert's son Neale, who began the bakery, purchased the lands of Pathhead farm, adjoining the estate, and then disposed of them in 1857 to the city of Glasgow for the formation of a park. The ground was laid out in the grand Victorian manner following designs of Sir Joseph Paxton, and was named the South Side Park. It was formally opened in September 1862 and was later renamed in honour of Queen Mary.

After the death of Neale Thomson, the house and estate were sold to the Trustees of Hutchesons' Hospital and for several years the house was rented by a lawyer, Andrew Hoggan. The estate

Camphill House may have been built by 'Mr Crawfurd of Posle' in 1777. This became the home of the Thomson family, owners of the Adelphi cotton mill in Hutchesontown and the Crossmyloof Bakery. The house has been recently converted to flats.

was bought by the Corporation of Glasgow and added to the park in 1894. The house was converted into a museum. In the 1980s there were plans to use the house as a Museum of Costume to display the city's 10,000 strong collection of historic costumes and accessories. This varied collection includes Flemish lace, Paisley shawls, Ayrshire embroidery, John Logie Baird's mother's wedding dress, and a black chiffon dress worn by Mrs David MacBrayne in 1905. Despite fund-raising efforts the project was not realised and the collection remains in store. Camphill House has now been restored and converted into nine flats.

Within the park are all-weather football pitches, a boating pond and two private bowling clubs. At the north end the Wellcroft Bowling Club can be identified by a W-shaped tree at the entrance. Wellcroft was founded in 1835 in Laurieston and moved to Queen's Park in 1876. Camphill Bowling Club at the south end of the park originated as a private green laid out by Andrew Hoggan for the use of his family, friends and estate workers. It became a club in 1888, with Andrew's son, John Hoggan, as first President, and James Glencairn Thomson as Vice-President. John Hoggan, a stock-broker, later moved to Rhu, and his house, Ardenvohr, later became the head-quarters of the Royal Northern and Clyde Yacht Club. The centenary of the Bowling Club was marked by the building of an extension to the clubhouse.

At the north-west corner of Queen's Park is one of the south side's finest churches, built to a design by William Leiper for a United Presbyterian congregation in 1878. Its elegant, soaring spire is a landmark in the district. This is the former Camphill-Queen's Park Church of Scotland, which closed in January 1995. The congregation of Queen's Park Baptist Church then acquired the building, and have carried out a major church refurbishment with the assistance of Historic Scotland.

Crossmyloof in the twentieth century: the Ice Rink

A traveller making his way from Glasgow to Pollokshaws around 1870 describes how on passing Regent Park Terrace at Strathbungo he sees a tall tenement of four storeys and attics looming ahead at the entrance to Crossmyloof, 'the colossal appearance of which dwarfs everything near it'. The traveller had just encountered Crossmyloof's first tenement, the cream-coloured building, today no 952 Pollokshaws Road. Another early tenement is the building with the name Campvale and the date 1873 on the north-west corner of Minard Road, then only a short street called Campvale Avenue.

Two fine examples of the red sandstone tenements which began to appear in the 1900s face the entrance to Camphill House. These are Springhill Gardens (1904) and Camphill Gate (1905), both built to the designs of John Nisbet and both allowed five storeys because of their open outlook over the park. Springhill Gardens is built round three sides of a square. Camphill Gate is the three tenement block with its name in 'Glasgow Style' lettering on the front of the building. Because there was no space for a back court here, a flat roof at first floor level was built for use as a drying area for washing. This feature is still in fairly common use at the backs of tenements further down Pollokshaws Road towards Shawlands. Another notable building of this great decade of expansion is the domed Glasgow Savings Bank (now TSB) at Shawlands Cross. The bank has a blue and white ceiling decorated with the coinage current when it was built in 1906.

Round the corner from the bank is the Waverley cinema, built in 1923, and once locally famous for its tearoom. Since 1973 the cinema has been a Bingo Hall. Two other cinemas in Shawlands, the Elephant and the Embassy, closed in the 1960s. Crossmyloof's best remembered attraction, however, was the Scottish Ice Rink. This was opened after many years of delay on 1 November 1907 by the President of the Royal Caledonian Curling Club, Sir Charles Dundas of Dunira. The rink was within a penny tram ride of the city centre and was also easily accessible from Crossmyloof station and quickly became one of the most frequented sports' centres in the west of Scotland. Several private skating and curling clubs made the rinks their headquarters, and the dining, tea and smoking rooms, all comfortably furnished and heated, were also open to the public. The rink closed during the First World War and remained closed until a new ice rink was built on the same site. This was opened in 1929 with accommodation for 3,000 skaters and spectators, six rinks and music to skate to provided by a live orchestra. Many Glaswegians have nostalgic memories of learning to skate on the hard ice at Crossmyloof. The rink was closed for good in 1986 and a Safeways supermarket now occupies the site.

FURTHER READING

General and Reference

Crawfurd, George, *General Description of the Shire of Renfrew,* 1710, continued by Semple, J, 1782, and by Robertson, G, 1810.

Wilson, John, *General View of the Agriculture of Renfrewshire,* 1812.

Senex (Robert Reid), *Glasgow Past and Present,* 1884.

Gibb, Andrew, Glasgow — *The Making of a City,* 1983.

Reed, Peter, Glasgow, *The Forming of the City,* 1993.

Fisher, Joe, *The Glasgow Enyclopedia,* 1994.

Edward, Mary, *Who Belongs to Glasgow?,* 1993.

Hume, J R, *The Industrial Archaeology of Glasgow,* 1974.

Gomme, A, and Walker, D, *Architecture of Glasgow,* rev. ed. 1987.

Worsdall, Frank, *The Tenement, A Way of Life,* 1979.

Macdonald, Hugh, *Rambles round Glasgow,* 1854.

Richardson, Thos., *Map of the town of Glasgow and country seven miles round,* 1795.

Cardonald

Kempsell, Alex., *The Golden Thumb: History of Washington Mills,* 1964.

Lindsay, Jean, *The Canals of Scotland,* 1968.

Innes , John A, *Old Cardonald had a Farm,* 1993.

Forsyth, J B, *Cardonald Parish Church, the first 100 Years,* 1989.

Lochhead, Alex., *The First Sixty Years: 30th Glasgow (Cardonald) Scout Troop,* 1909–1969, 1969.

Cathcart

Gartshore, Alex., *Cathcart Memories,* 1938.

Marshall, Jean, *Why Cathcart,* 3rd ed., 1972.

Reader, Wm J, *The Weir Group: centenary history,* 1971.

Kernahan, Jack, *The Cathcart Circle,* 1980.

Gorbals

Ord J, *The Story of the Barony of Gorbals,* 1919.

Bell, Gilbert T, (Gorbals History Research Group), *Third Time Lucky,* 1994.

Collins, Kenneth E, *Second City Jewry,* 1990.

Hutt C and Caplan, H, *A Scottish Shtehl: Jewish Life in the Gorbals,* 1880–1974, 1974.

Coveney, Michael, *The Citz: 21 years of the Glasgow Citizens' Theatre,* 1990.

Dunlop, A C, *Hutchesons' Grammar: History of a Glasgow School,* 1992.

Govan

Brotchie, T C F, *History of Govan,* 1905.
Transactions of Old Govan Club, 1914–1934.
Ritchie, Anna (ed.), *Govan and its Early Medieval Sculpture,* 1994.
Moss, M, and Hume, J, *Workshop of the British Empire,* 1977.
Walker, Frank M, *Song of the Clyde: A History of Clyde Shipbuilding,* 1984.
Simpson, John, *Govan's Maritime Past,* 1988.
Donnelly, Patrick, *Govan on the Clyde,* 1994.
Rountree, George, *A Govan Childhood: the nineteen thirties,* 1993.

Govanhill and Polmadie

Eunson, Eric, *Old Govanhill,* 1994.
Woods, P, *Third Lanark Football Club,* 1981.
Nicolson, M, and O'Neill, M, *Glasgow: Locomotive Builder to the World, 1987.*
Macmillan, Nigel, *Locomotive Apprentice at the North British Locomotive Co,* 1992.

Hurlet and Nitshill

Taylor, Charles, *Levern Delineated,* 1831.
Murray, Robert, *Annals of Barrhead,* 1942.
Hughson, Irene (ed.), *Bygone Barrhead.*
Bellarmine Resource Centre, various papers.

Langside

Scott, A M, 'The Battle of Langside' in *Transactions of the Glasgow Archaeological Society,* 1885–90.
Slater, S D and Dow, D A, *The Victoria Infirmay of Glasgow 1890–1990, A Centenary History,* 1990.
Greene, Margaret, *From Langside to Battlefield,* n.d.

Pollokshaws

McCallum, Andrew, *Pollokshaws Village and Burgh,* 1600–1912, 1925.
Milton, Nan, *John Maclean,* 1973.
McLean, Iain, *The Legend of Red Clydeside,* 1983.
Fraser, William, *Memoirs of the Maxwells of Pollok,* 1863.

Strathbungo and Crossmyloof

Scott, A M, 'Notes on the village of Strathbungo', in *Transactions of the Glasgow Archaeological Society,* 1885–90.
MacMillan, Archibald, *Jeems Kaye, his adventures and opinions,* 1903.
McFadzean, Ronald, *Life and Work of Alexander Thomson,* 1979.
Munro, John M, *Strathbungo and its Kirk,* 1933.
Steven, Rev Keith M, *Queen's Park West Church of Scotland, a Centenary History,* 1967.

INDEX